JOSHUA
and
JUDGES

J. Vernon McGee

THOMAS NELSON PUBLISHERS

Nashville

Published in Nashville, Tennessee, by Thomas Nelson, Inc., and distributed in Canada by Lawson Falle, Ltd., Cambridge, Ontario.

Excerpts from *The New Scofield Reference Bible, King James Version*, copyright © 1967 by Oxford University Press, Inc., are reprinted by permission.

Scripture quotations are from the KING JAMES VERSION of the Bible.

Library of Congress Cataloging-in-Publication Data

McGee, J. Vernon (John Vernon), 1904–1988
   [Thru the Bible with J. Vernon McGee]
   Thru the Bible commentary series / J. Vernon McGee.
     p.   cm.
   Reprint. Originally published: Thru the Bible with J. Vernon McGee. 1975.
   Includes bibliographical references.
   ISBN 0-8407-3260-0
   1. Bible—Commentaries. I. Title.
BS491.2.M37 1991
220.7′7—dc20   90–41340
                                       CIP

Printed in the United States of America
1 2 3 4 5 6 7 — 96 95 94 93 92 91

CONTENTS

JOSHUA

JUDGES

PREFACE

The radio broadcasts of the Thru the Bible Radio five-year program were transcribed, edited, and published first in single-volume paperbacks to accommodate the radio audience.

There has been a minimal amount of further editing for this publication. Therefore, these messages are not the word-for-word recording of the taped messages which went out over the air. The changes were necessary to accommodate a reading audience rather than a listening audience.

These are popular messages, prepared originally for a radio audience. They should not be considered a commentary on the entire Bible in any sense of that term. These messages are devoid of any attempt to present a theological or technical commentary on the Bible. Behind these messages is a great deal of research and study in order to interpret the Bible from a popular rather than from a scholarly (and too-often boring) viewpoint.

We have definitely and deliberately attempted "to put the cookies on the bottom shelf so that the kiddies could get them."

The fact that these messages have been translated into many languages for radio broadcasting and have been received with enthusiasm reveals the need for a simple teaching of the whole Bible for the masses of the world.

I am indebted to many people and to many sources for bringing this volume into existence. I should express my especial thanks to my secretary, Gertrude Cutler, who supervised the editorial work; to Dr. Elliott R. Cole, my associate, who handled all the detailed work with the publishers; and finally, to my wife Ruth for tenaciously encouraging me from the beginning to put my notes and messages into printed form.

Solomon wrote, ". . . of making many books there is no end; and much study is a weariness of the flesh" (Eccl. 12:12). On a sea of books that flood the marketplace, we launch this series of THRU THE BIBLE with the hope that it might draw many to the one Book, *The Bible*.

J. VERNON McGEE

JOSHUA

The Book of

JOSHUA

INTRODUCTION

In the Book of Genesis Israel was born. In the Book of Exodus Israel was chosen. In the Book of Numbers the nation was proven. In the Book of Leviticus it was brought nigh by the blood. In Deuteronomy it was instructed. Now in the Book of Joshua it faces conflict and conquest.

The Book of Joshua completes the redemption of Israel that was begun in Exodus. Exodus is the book of redemption *out* of Egypt; Joshua is the book of redemption *into* the Promised Land.

The key word in the Book of Joshua is *possession*. God had given the children of Israel their land in an unconditional covenant. To Abraham He had said, "And I will give unto thee, and to thy seed after thee, the land wherein thou art a stranger, all the land of Canaan, for an everlasting possession; and I will be their God" (Gen. 17:8). However, Israel's possession of the land was conditional. There was conflict and there was conquest. They had to fight battles and lay hold of their possessions. And, as Joshua reminded them in his final message before his death, their obedience to the Word of God would determine their continued possession of the land.

The Talmud says that Joshua wrote all but the concluding five verses, which were written by Phinehas. Joshua was the successor to Moses. He was a great general. Born a slave in Egypt, he was forty years old at the time of the Exodus out of Egypt. He was eighty years old when he received his commission as Moses' successor and one hundred ten years old at his death. Joshua had already gained prominence during the wilderness wanderings. When they were attacked by the army of Amalek, it was Joshua who organized the men into an army that fought off Amalek. Joshua served as a minister or servant to Moses. References to him in that connection reveal his loyalty to Moses and his devotion to God. At Kadesh-barnea he was one of the twelve men who went to spy out the land of Canaan. He is one of the two spies that returned with a favorable report in full confidence that God would give them the land.

Joshua's name means "Jehovah saves." The same word in the New Testament is *Jesus*. Joshua was a man of courage, dependence upon God, faith, leadership, enthusiasm, and fidelity. He is a type of Christ in his name and in his work. As another has said, "Joshua shows that a man of average ability may become a leader in the church. Joshua received his call not in flaming letters written across the sky, but from an older man who knew God and knew Joshua, and saw that he was fitted by God to be a leader."

The Book of Joshua has a very practical application to the believer today. The Promised Land cannot be a type of heaven since heaven is not a place of conflict and conquest. Heaven is received as a gift of the grace of God. Rather, the Promised Land represents the place to which believers are brought right here in this world today. The Book of Joshua corresponds to the Epistle to the Ephesians in the New Testament where we see that the believer is blessed with all spiritual blessings. The practical possession and experience of them depends upon conflict and conquest. These are never attained through the energy of the flesh, but through the power of the Holy Spirit in the yielded life of the believer. The Book of Joshua is the pattern, and it illustrates the method by which the believer can possess what God has given to him.

OUTLINE

I. Land Entered, Chapters 1—12
A. Commission and Command of Joshua, Chapter 1
B. Contact of Spies with Rahab, Chapter 2
C. Crossing the Jordan River, Chapter 3
D. Construction of Two Memorials, Chapter 4
E. Conditioned for Conquest, Chapter 5
F. Center of Land Attacked, Chapters 6—8
    1. Conquest of Jericho, Chapter 6
    2. Conquest of Ai, Chapters 7—8
G. Campaign in the South, Chapters 9—10
    1. Compact with the Gibeonites, Chapter 9
    2. Conquest of Five Kings of Amorites, Chapter 10
    (Miracle of sun)
H. Campaign in the North, Chapter 11
   (Conclusion of Joshua's leadership in war)
I. Conquered Kings Listed, Chapter 12

II. Land Divided, Chapters 13—22
A. Command of Joshua Is Terminated;
   Confirmation of Land to the Two and One-half Tribes,
   Chapter 13
B. Caleb Given Hebron, Chapter 14
C. Consignment of Land to the Tribes of Israel, Chapters
   15—19
D. Cities of Refuge, Chapter 20
E. Cities for Levites, Chapter 21
F. Command to the Two and One-half Tribes to Return Home;
   Construction of Altar to "See To," Chapter 22

III. Last Message of Joshua, Chapters 23—24
A. Call to Leaders of Israel for Courage and Certainty,
   Chapter 23

CHAPTER 1

THEME: Commission and command of Joshua

In the first twelve chapters of Joshua the Promised Land is entered. Then in chapters 13—21 we see the land divided. The book concludes with the final message of Joshua to his people.

The great theme of Joshua is *possession.* In this first chapter we will see what is meant by that.

The chapter opens with the Lord personally giving Joshua his commission and his command.

> Now after the death of Moses the servant of the LORD it came to pass, that the LORD spake unto Joshua the son of Nun, Moses' minister, saying [Josh. 1:1].

The first word of this verse, *Now,* should be translated "And," which connects it with the final chapter of Deuteronomy. *And* is a connective. The minute a speaker says *and,* he has to keep talking because *and* connects something that has gone before with something that is coming. This supports the theory that Deuteronomy 34 was written by Joshua.

> Moses my servant is dead; now therefore arise, go over this Jordan, thou, and all this people, unto the land which I do give to them, even to the children of Israel [Josh. 1:2].

"Moses my servant is dead." As we have seen, Moses was not essential to lead the children of Israel into the land. In fact, he could not bring them into the Land of Promise. Moses represented the Law and the Law cannot save us. The Law is a revealer and not a redeemer. It shows us that we are sinners. The Law was never a savior. Moses could not lead Israel into the land because of his failure. The problem was not

with the Law but with Moses just as the problem is with us. The Law
reveals that we have fallen short of the glory of God. "Moses my servant is dead." Only Jesus our Savior, our Joshua, can lead us into the
place of blessing He has for us.

This verse tells us that the land was given to Israel. Israel's ownership was unconditional. God promised it to Abraham and his off-
spring. God reaffirmed His promise again and again in the Book of
Genesis. In the Book of Deuteronomy God made the Palestinian covenant with Israel which gave them the land as an everlasting possession.

**Every place that the sole of your foot shall tread upon,
that have I given unto you, as I said unto Moses [Josh.
1:3].**

God has given them the land. The land is theirs, but their enjoyment of
it depends upon their taking possession of it. That part of the land
upon which they walked would belong to them. Comparatively speaking, we have been told in Ephesians 1:3 that we are blessed with all
spiritual blessings in the heavenlies. Unfortunately, very few Christians lay hold of the spiritual blessings that belong to them.

Years ago a certain Englishman moved to the United States. Soon
after he arrived he dropped out of sight. One day his uncle in England
died and left him about a five-million dollar estate. Scotland Yard
went about trying to locate the man whose last address had been in
Chicago. They searched for him but never found him. Later I heard
that he was found one morning frozen to death in an entryway of a
cheap hotel. He could not afford twenty-five cents for a room although
he was heir to five million dollars! He did not claim what was his. He
did not lay hold of what belonged to him.

Although God gave Israel the Promised Land, they never possessed
all of it. As a matter of fact, Israel got very little of the land. Many
Christians today are like Israel in that they are blessed with all spiritual blessings and yet they die like bums in a doorway without claiming those blessings as their own. What a tragedy that is. The Book of
Joshua is going to tell us how to lay hold of our possessions. Because

there will be conflict, we are told in Ephesians 6 to put on the whole armor of God. We have a spiritual enemy fighting against us. "For we wrestle not against flesh and blood, but against principalities, against powers, against the rulers of the darkness of this world, against spiritual wickedness in high places" (Eph. 6:12). Ours is a spiritual enemy.

We will have to wear the whole armor of God. The victory has to be won. However, you and I don't get the victory; the Lord Jesus Christ gets the victory. We will get what Israel got—deliverance and possessions. Every victory Israel gained was given by God. If you and I ever win a victory, He will win it for us. We will, by faith, enter into these wonderful possessions.

> **From the wilderness and this Lebanon even unto the great river, the river Euphrates, all the land of the Hittites, and unto the great sea toward the going down of the sun, shall be your coast [Josh. 1:4].**

God gave Israel 300,000 square miles of land and the most they ever claimed was 30,000 square miles. They did not do very well, did they? They took possession of about one-tenth of what God had given them. That is about the same amount of spiritual possessions claimed by believers today.

> **There shall not any man be able to stand before thee all the days of thy life: as I was with Moses, so I will be with thee: I will not fail thee, nor forsake thee [Josh. 1:5].**

Joshua, average man that he was, needed to be encouraged. God encouraged him here in a most wonderful way. God says, "I won't desert you. Just as I was with Moses, I'll be with you."

> **Be strong and of a good courage: for unto this people shalt thou divide for an inheritance the land, which I sware unto their fathers to give them.**

> Only be thou strong and very courageous, that thou
> mayest observe to do according to all the law, which
> Moses my servant commanded thee: turn not from it to
> the right hand or to the left, that thou mayest prosper
> whithersoever thou goest [Josh. 1:6-7].

Twice God says to him, "Be strong and of a good courage." He is encouraging him.

Now notice something that is all important:

> This book of the law shall not depart out of thy mouth;
> but thou shalt meditate therein day and night, that thou
> mayest observe to do according to all that is written
> therein: for then thou shalt make thy way prosperous,
> and then thou shalt have good success [Josh. 1:8].

There were no written Scriptures before Moses, and God communi-
cated to Moses by speaking with him face to face. But Moses had faith-
fully recorded all that God had given to him so that the first five books
of the Bible were available to Joshua and the people of Israel. In it God
had given them all they needed to know to enter the land. They were
not to depart from it. They were to meditate on it and observe to do it.

> Have not I commanded thee? Be strong and of a good
> courage; be not afraid, neither be thou dismayed: for the
> LORD thy God is with thee whithersoever thou goest
> [Josh. 1:9].

Joshua is to take the Word of God in one hand and a sword in the other.
He is to move out by faith. God encourages him again to be strong and
courageous.

Friends, like Joshua, we as believers need to be strong and courageous. We need to possess our spiritual possessions by faith. Remember we are in enemy territory.

> Then Joshua commanded the officers of the people, say-
> ing [Josh. 1:10].

Joshua took charge, and he didn't do it by presumption but in confidence. He did it because God told him to do it.

God had told Moses He would be with him. When Moses returned to Egypt, after spending years in Midian, he was fearful, but God said, "Now therefore go, and I will be with thy mouth, and teach thee what thou shalt say" (Exod. 4:12). This is God's method. When God called Jeremiah in a dark and difficult day, He said, "And they shall fight against thee; but they shall not prevail against thee; for I am with thee, saith the LORD, to deliver thee" (Jer. 1:19). We need the kind of conviction and courage spoken about in Hebrews 13:6, "So that we may boldly say, The Lord is my helper, and I will not fear what man shall do unto me." When David first said these words, which were quoted in Hebrews from Psalm 118:6, he turned his mind and heart away from that which was seen to that which was unseen. It means that he became occupied with the living and true God. He recognized the spiritual bond that was between him and the Lord. His soul was "bound up in a bundle of life with God." He could say, "The Lord is my helper." David knew that the Lord could deliver him.

Joshua believed God. God had encouraged him and told him to step out. The Word of God was to be his authority. It was not to depart out of his mouth. He was to meditate on it. He was to do what was written in the Word. That is the formula of faith.

> **Pass through the host, and command the people, saying, Prepare you victuals; for within three days ye shall pass over this Jordan, to go in to possess the land, which the LORD your God giveth you to possess it [Josh. 1:11].**

Israel's ownership of the land is unconditional, but Israel's possession of it is conditional. Israel had to take the land. The key word of the Book of Joshua is not *victory*—it is God who gets the victory. The key word is *possession*. Israel was to possess the land.

A little later on, when Israel got into the land, the manna ceased and they ate the old corn of the land. That would be corn they captured from the enemy, old corn, because they hadn't had a chance to grow it. As you recall, they had to gather manna every day. Manna would not keep. If it was kept for more than one day, it became unfit to eat. The children of Israel had to gather manna every morning. That is why we are told in Ephesians 5:18 to be filled with the Spirit. Being filled with the Spirit is not a one-time job. You do not go to the gas station once and tell the attendant to fill up your tank and then seal the tank because you will never need more gas. That would be presumption. In fact, it would be foolish and stupid. There are many Christians, however, who think that they can have one experience and that is it. My friend, if you are going to walk with Him and live for Him, you will need a *daily* filling of the Holy Spirit of God. In fact, since you fill up the physical man three times a day, it would not be a bad idea to fill up the spiritual man three times a day. We all need a constant filling of the Holy Spirit, a looking to Him, and a resting upon Him.

And to the Reubenites, and to the Gadites, and to half the tribe of Manasseh, spake Joshua, saying [Josh. 1:12].

These two and one-half tribes did not cross over the river to settle there, and we find their defection very early. Moses was still alive when they came to the east bank of the Jordan, and you will find that they made a request recorded in Numbers 32:1–2, 5: "Now the children of Reuben and the children of Gad had a very great multitude of cattle: and when they saw the land of Jazer, and the land of Gilead, that, behold, the place was a place for cattle; the children of Gad and the children of Reuben came and spake unto Moses, and to Eleazar the priest . . . saying . . . Wherefore, . . . if we have found grace in thy sight, let this land be given unto thy servants for a possession, and bring us not over Jordan." This was the specific request of two and one-half tribes. They were asking for land on the wrong side of the Jordan River.

Remember the word which Moses the servant of the LORD commanded you, saying, The LORD your God hath given you rest, and hath given you this land.

> Your wives, your little ones, and your cattle, shall re-
> main in the land which Moses gave you on this side Jor-
> dan; but ye shall pass before your brethren armed, all
> the mighty men of valour, and help them;
>
> Until the LORD have given your brethren rest, as he hath
> given you, and they also have possessed the land which
> the LORD your God giveth them: then ye shall return
> unto the land of your possession, and enjoy it, which
> Moses the LORD'S servant gave you on this side Jordan
> toward the sunrising [Josh. 1:13-15].

Joshua is reminding them that Moses had given them permission to
live on the east side of Jordan on the condition that their army would
help the other tribes possess their land on the west of the river. This
they agree to do.

> And they answered Joshua, saying, All that thou com-
> mandest us we will do, and whithersoever thou sendest
> us, we will go.
>
> According as we hearkened unto Moses in all things, so
> will we hearken unto thee: only the LORD thy God be
> with thee, as he was with Moses.
>
> Whosoever he be that doth rebel against thy command-
> ment, and will not hearken unto thy words in all that
> thou commandest him, he shall be put to death: only be
> strong and of a good courage [Josh. 1:16-18].

Perhaps you are asking the questions, Well, what is wrong with dwelling on the east side of the River Jordan? Is it so essential to cross over
the river? Is not the east bank of the Jordan River part of the Promised
Land? Such questions are pertinent and require that we look at the
passage of Scripture in which lies the account of the crossing of the
Jordan River, which we will do shortly.

Crossing the Jordan River was symbolic of the death and resurrection of Jesus Christ. Under no condition, however, does it set forth our

physical death. We often sing the old song, "On Jordan's Stormy Banks I Stand." To begin with, that is not a stormy stream; neither do you and I stand on the stormy banks. Christ alone was nailed to that cross and, hanging there, bore all the storms of the judgment of sin. When the storms of judgment fell on Him, they fell on us. The River Jordan speaks of *sanctification*, and the death of Christ was for our sanctification.

In the Book of Judges we find out that the two and one-half tribes made a big mistake staying on the wrong side of Jordan. Also, when Christ crossed the Sea of Galilee and came to the country of the Gadarenes, He found the Jews in the pig business. They started off wrong on the wrong side of the Jordan River.

Many Christians are in the pig business today and are frustrated. They ought to enter into the rest He has provided in His death and resurrection.

CHAPTER 2

THEME: Contact of spies with Rahab

Here we are introduced to a woman, a very shady character. She was a prostitute, and her name is Rahab. The remarkable fact is that in the New Testament she is listed with those who are commonly called the heroes of faith. "By faith the harlot Rahab perished not with them that believed not, when she had received the spies with peace" (Heb. 11:31). I do not like to think of Hebrews 11 as a record of *heroes* of faith because that puts the emphasis on humanity. I like to put the emphasis upon faith. The men and women recorded there illustrate what faith did in all ages under all circumstances in their lives. For us it means that faith can do the same thing for us, seeing "we also are compassed about with so great a cloud of witnesses" (Heb. 12:1).

Another startling fact is that Rahab is in the genealogy of Christ! The New Testament opens with that genealogy, and you don't read five verses of the New Testament until you come to this woman's name. How did she get into the genealogy of Christ? She got there by faith.

As you can see, the chapter before us introduces a remarkable woman.

> **And Joshua the son of Nun sent out of Shittim two men to spy secretly, saying, Go view the land, even Jericho. And they went, and came into an harlot's house, named Rahab, and lodged there [Josh. 2:1].**

Notice that two spies are sent in. You may be thinking that this is another mistake. Earlier they had sent the spies to see if they could take the land. Now they are being sent, not to see if they can take the land, but to find the best way to enter the land. The purpose is entirely different, you see.

Rahab, a citizen of Jericho, opens her home to the spies.

And it was told the king of Jericho, saying, Behold, there came men in hither tonight of the children of Israel to search out the country.

And the king of Jericho sent unto Rahab, saying, Bring forth the men that are come to thee, which are entered into thine house: for they be come to search out all the country.

And the woman took the two men, and hid them, and said thus, There came men unto me, but I wist not whence they were:

And it came to pass about the time of shutting of the gate, when it was dark, that the men went out: whither the men went I wot not: pursue after them quickly; for ye shall overtake them.

But she had brought them up to the roof of the house, and hid them with the stalks of flax, which she had laid in order upon the roof.

And the men pursued after them the way to Jordan unto the fords: and as soon as they which pursued after them were gone out, they shut the gate [Josh. 2:2–7].

She told her king an outright lie to protect these men. And in doing so, she actually jeopardized her own life. Now why would she put her life on the line like this? She didn't have to. She is in a business, by the way, where anything goes. Why did she lie to her own people and protect the enemy?

Before we see the answer to that question, let me raise another question. Is it possible to condone Rahab's action? Scripture is very clear on the fact that we, as children of God, are to obey authority and those that have the rule over us. Rahab certainly did not do that. I do not think we could call her a child of God until sometime after this experience. That would be one explanation. However, there is another explanation that I consider meaningful to us today.

A believer should certainly obey the authorities and those who have rule over us. A Christian should be the most law-abiding citizen in the land. But when the laws of a state conflict with God's revealed will, then the Christian has no choice but to obey the command of God. This was the experience of Peter and John when the authorities attempted to silence them in their witness for Christ, ". . . Whether it be right in the sight of God to hearken unto you more than unto God, judge ye. For we cannot but speak the things which we have seen and heard" (Acts 4:19–20). The believer is to obey the Word of God today rather than the word of man. That should be our attitude as children of God.

Now we will let Rahab answer our first question: why did she lie to protect the enemy?

> **And before they were laid down, she came up unto them upon the roof;**
>
> **And she said unto the men, I know that the LORD hath given you the land, and that your terror is fallen upon us, and that all the inhabitants of the land faint because of you [Josh. 2:8–9].**

She gives an insight into the thinking of the Canaanites at that time. The word is out that a great company of people is coming into that land. They believe they are going to take the land. The population is stirred up, and they are afraid. This is the report that Rahab gives the spies. I guess she was in a position to get all the gossip, and she could see that all of her people were terrified because of Israel's advance.

> **For we have heard how the LORD dried up the water of the Red sea for you, when ye came out of Egypt; and what ye did unto the two kings of the Amorites, that were on the other side Jordan, Sihon and Og, whom ye utterly destroyed [Josh. 2:10].**

Notice: "We have heard how the LORD dried up the water of the Red sea for you." How long ago was this? That happened forty years before they

arrived at the Jordan River! During those forty years God had been giving the people of Canaan an opportunity to turn to Him. How do we
know that? Because God had said to Abraham that his seed would be
strangers in a foreign land for 400 years; then in the fourth generation
they would come again because ". . . the iniquity of the Amorites is not
yet full" (Gen. 15:16). That was 420 years before this. In other words,
God was going to give the people of Canaan 420 years to decide
whether or not they would turn to Him.

The critic declares that the God of the Old Testament was a great
big bully, that He was cruel and barbaric. When God gave the people of
Canaan 420 years to repent, in my opinion, that is long enough. But
God extended the time by forty more years and saw to it that they heard
how He had revealed Himself by delivering His people from Egypt.
God did not destroy a people that had not heard about Him. He gave
them ample opportunity to turn to Him. My question, Mr. Critic, is—
how much longer do you think God should have given them?

In the New Testament God has not changed. He has made it very
clear that those who reject Jesus Christ are going to hell. Does it shock
you to hear that in this very "civilized" society that discounts the existence of hell? When God's judgment falls, I am sure there will be some
soft-hearted and soft-headed folk on the sideline who will say, "He
should have given them more time." More time? My friend, over 1900
years have gone by. God is patient; He is slow to anger; He is merciful.
How much longer do you want Him to give us? He has been giving the
world ample opportunity to turn to Christ.

The harlot said, "We have heard." And notice the reaction.

**And as soon as we had heard these things, our hearts
did melt, neither did there remain any more courage in
any man, because of you: for the LORD your God, he is
God in heaven above, and in earth beneath [Josh. 2:11].**

Not only did they hear this, but they knew it was true. Even so, they
did not turn to God.

There are a great many people today who know as a historical fact
that Jesus Christ died, was buried, and rose again, but they are not

saved. What saves you? It is trusting Him as your personal Savior. It is
to have a personal relationship with Him.

Now that's not all Rahab said.

> Now therefore, I pray you, swear unto me by the LORD,
> since I have shewed you kindness, that ye will also shew
> kindness unto my father's house, and give me a true
> token:
>
> And that ye will save alive my father, and my mother,
> and my brethren, and my sisters, and all that they have,
> and deliver our lives from death.
>
> And the men answered her, Our life for yours, if ye utter
> not this our business. And it shall be, when the LORD
> hath given us the land, that we will deal kindly and
> truly with thee [Josh. 2:12–14].

She not only believed, but she is acting on that belief. This is her reason for putting her life in jeopardy to protect enemy spies. She heard;
she believed; then she acted upon her belief.

This is salvation, friend. When you hear the Gospel, the good news
of what Christ has done for you, you must not only believe it as a historical fact, you must trust Christ yourself.

So this woman trusted the fact that God was going to give them that
land. She turned to the living and true God. "By faith the harlot Rahab
perished not with them that believed not, when she had received the
spies with peace" (Heb. 11:31).

The spies promise to spare all of her family that is with her in the
house when Jericho is attacked.

> Behold, when we come into the land, thou shalt bind
> this line of scarlet thread in the window which thou
> didst let us down by: and thou shalt bring thy father, and
> thy mother, and thy brethren, and all thy father's house-
> hold, home unto thee [Josh. 2:18].

And if the king of the city of Jericho had turned to God, he would have been saved. In fact, the whole city could have been spared if they had believed in God.

Now we will look at the final verses of this chapter, the report of the spies.

> **So the two men returned, and descended from the mountain, and passed over, and came to Joshua the son of Nun, and told him all things that befell them:**
>
> **And they said unto Joshua, Truly the LORD hath delivered into our hands all the land; for even all the inhabitants of the country do faint because of us [Josh. 2:23–24].**

You see, the spies' report is entirely different from the spies who went into the land forty years earlier. It is not a question now whether or not they will go into the land. They *are* going in. "All the inhabitants of the country do faint because of us" is the information they got from Rahab the harlot.

CHAPTER 3

THEME: Crossing the Jordan River

Crossing the Jordan River into the land of Canaan was a major turning point as far as the faith of the Israelites was concerned. Almost forty years earlier the children of Israel had faced a similar crisis, but they had failed. To slip away into the wilderness of Sinai by crossing the Red Sea required some faith. However, to invade the land of Canaan by crossing the Jordan River took a great deal more faith because, having once crossed the river, there would be no possibility of escape. Once in the land, they would have to face the enemy with their armies, chariots, and walled cities. The entire nation took this step together in complete commitment to God.

> **And Joshua rose early in the morning; and they removed from Shittim, and came to Jordan, he and all the children of Israel, and lodged there before they passed over.**
>
> **And it came to pass after three days, that the officers went through the host;**
>
> **And they commanded the people, saying, When ye see the ark of the covenant of the LORD your God, and the priests the Levites bearing it, then ye shall remove from your place, and go after it.**
>
> **Yet there shall be a space between you and it, about two thousand cubits by measure: come not near unto it, that ye may know the way by which ye must go: for ye have not passed this way heretofore [Josh. 3:1–4].**

God commanded Joshua and the children of Israel to cross over the Jordan River. When they went over the Jordan River, it was quite different from their crossing the Red Sea. When they crossed the Red Sea,

Moses went down to the water and smote it with his rod. All that night the waters rolled back. But when they crossed the Jordan River, it was actually a greater miracle, for it was at flood stage and their crossing caused a holding back of the waters that were rushing to the Dead Sea.

Also something new has been added. The ark is to go down far ahead of the people, three thousand feet, which is almost a mile; and it is to be carried by priests who are to come to the edge of the Jordan River and stand there.

> **And as they that bare the ark were come unto Jordan,**
> **and the feet of the priests that bare the ark were dipped**
> **in the brim of the water, (for Jordan overfloweth all his**
> **banks all the time of harvest,) [Josh. 3:15].**

When the priests came to the edge of the Jordan River, the flow of water was restrained as if a dam had been put over it. The waters that were this side of it passed on down, and before long there was a dry passage. This is one of the greatest miracles recorded in Scripture.

This was the spring of the year. That land had two rainy seasons: in the fall and in the spring. The spring rains were most abundant. The Jordan was at flood stage. It is entirely possible that the people on the west side of Jordan felt that they had several days, or maybe several weeks, before the Israelites could get across the river. They probably felt that there was no immediate danger. Some of them, however, may have had a lurking fear, knowing that forty years earlier these people had crossed the Red Sea.

> **That the waters which came down from above stood and**
> **rose up upon an heap very far from the city Adam, that**
> **is beside Zaretan: and those that came down toward the**
> **sea of the plain, even the salt sea, failed, and were cut**
> **off: and the people passed over right against Jericho.**

> **And the priests that bare the ark of the covenant of the**
> **LORD stood firm on dry ground in the midst of Jordan,**
> **and all the Israelites passed over on dry ground, until**

all the people were passed clean over Jordan [Josh. 3:16–17].

Note that the priests moved to the center of the Jordan River and stood there holding the ark until all of the children of Israel had passed over. The Israelites crossed the river at Jericho, but the waters were dammed up way back to the city of Adam. Now I have never been able to locate the city of Adam. What is the meaning of this city? Well, friend, it is the city we all came from in the sense that Adam is the father of the human family and by Adam came death. What was taking place at the Jordan River represented the death and resurrection of Christ and His work on the cross. It not only reached forward over 1,900 years to where you and I are, but it also reached back to Adam and the beginning of the human family. That is the picture we have here.

Now the ark is one of the finest types of the Lord Jesus Christ given in the Old Testament, although there are several that are conspicuous and outstanding. The ark had been in the very heart of Israel's camp for forty years during the wilderness march. Every night when they came into camp, the entire twelve tribes of Israel camped about the ark. It was the very center. But now, for the first time, that which speaks of Christ goes ahead to the Jordan River and enters it first.

As has already been stated, Christ goes before us in death. Of course He goes with us in life—as we pass through this world, He is with us. But He went before us in death; and when our Lord entered death, He entered it for you and for me.

CHAPTER 4

THEME: Construction of two memorials

Twelve men are appointed to take twelve stones out of the Jordan River, and twelve other stones are set up in the midst of the Jordan River as a memorial. The priests carrying the ark pass over the river, and the water of the river returns to its normal flow. God magnifies Joshua.

> And it came to pass, when all the people were clean passed over Jordan, that the LORD spake unto Joshua, saying,
>
> Take you twelve men out of the people, out of every tribe a man,
>
> And command ye them, saying, Take you hence out of the midst of Jordan, out of the place where the priests' feet stood firm, twelve stones, and ye shall carry them over with you, and leave them in the lodging place, where ye shall lodge this night [Josh. 4:1–3].

This is something that they did. And here is what happened.

> And the children of Israel did so as Joshua commanded, and took up twelve stones out of the midst of Jordan, as the LORD spake unto Joshua, according to the number of the tribes of the children of Israel, and carried them over with them unto the place where they lodged, and laid them down there [Josh. 4:8].

The twelve stones taken out of Jordan and put on the west bank of the river were a reminder of God's tremendous power on Israel's behalf.

> And Joshua set up twelve stones in the midst of Jordan,
> in the place where the feet of the priests which bare the
> ark of the covenant stood: and they are there unto this
> day [Josh. 4:9].

That is, the stones were there when Joshua wrote this record.

Now this section has great spiritual significance for us today. In an attempt to get the full significance of this, I am quoting from Phillips' book (which is not a translation, but is an interpretation), Romans 6:1-4: "Now what is our response to be? Shall we sin to our heart's content and see how far we can exploit the grace of God? What a ghastly thought! We, who have died to sin—how could we live in sin a moment longer?" Now when did we die to sin? "Have you forgotten that all of us who were baptized into Jesus Christ were, by that very action, sharing in his death? We were dead and buried with him in baptism, so that just as he was raised from the dead by the splendid revelation of the Father's power so we too might rise to life on a new plane altogether." My friend, may I say to you that Christ went unto death for you and me, and that is set before us here in the Book of Joshua. Twelve stones were put into the water of death. Those twelve stones were placed in Jordan to speak of the death of Christ. And the twelve stones taken out of Jordan and put on the west bank represent the resurrection of Christ.

The Lord Jesus Christ died over 1,900 years ago, and Paul makes it clear in the sixth chapter of Romans that we are *identified* with Him in His death. It is too bad that the word *baptize* was transliterated and not translated. It is a Greek word *baptizo*, and its primary meaning here has no connection with water. It speaks of identification. We are identified with Christ in His death; and when He died, my friend, He died for us. His death was our death. When He arose from the dead, then we arose from the dead. And we are joined today to a living Christ. It is only in the measure that we are joined to Him that you and I can enjoy all spiritual blessings. I trust that you realize that. We have become identified with Him!

Now, when the children of Israel crossed over the river, they became citizens of Palestine. They became forever identified with that land—so much so, that today, even at this hour, they speak of the Jew in Palestine. And when he is out of that land, he is spoken of as the "wandering Jew." Let us tie this fact up with another great fact: When you, my friend, came to Christ and accepted Him as your Savior, His death became your death and His resurrection your resurrection. When you "wander" from this identity, even briefly, think of the tragic meaning.

Paul wrote a blessed truth to the Ephesians: "But God, who is rich in mercy, for his great love wherewith he loved us, Even when we were dead in sins, hath quickened us together with Christ, (by grace ye are saved;) And hath raised us up together, and made us sit together in heavenly places in Christ Jesus: That in the ages to come he might shew the exceeding riches of his grace in his kindness toward us through Christ Jesus" (Eph. 2:4–7). When He died, He died for your sin that you might have life; and when He came back from the dead, His life was then your life. Now you are joined to the living God. My friend, that is one of the great truths of the Word of God.

> **And the people came up out of Jordan on the tenth day of the first month, and encamped in Gilgal, in the east border of Jericho.**
>
> **And those twelve stones, which they took out of Jordan, did Joshua pitch in Gilgal.**
>
> **And he spake unto the children of Israel, saying, When your children shall ask their fathers in time to come, saying, What mean these stones?**
>
> **Then ye shall let your children know, saying, Israel came over this Jordan on dry land [Josh. 4:19–22].**

If we carry the spiritual lesson out in this passage, our conclusion can only be that we are to teach our children the Gospel. The business of parents is to give their children the Gospel. There is no privilege like that of a parent leading his child to a saving knowledge of Christ. My wife had the privilege of leading our daughter to the Lord. This is the responsibility of parents.

For the LORD your God dried up the waters of Jordan from before you, until ye were passed over, as the LORD your God did to the Red sea, which he dried up from before us, until we were gone over:

That all the people of the earth might know the hand of the LORD, that it is mighty: that ye might fear the LORD your God for ever [Josh. 23–24].

What God did for the children of Israel He did for their benefit, your benefit, and mine. He did it that all the people of the earth might know that the hand of the Lord is indeed mighty. This purpose was graphically fulfilled as soon as the Canaanites heard the news that the children of Israel had crossed over Jordan.

Some of the important things to remember in this chapter are that the ark goes before and divides the Jordan River—not the rod of Moses. The ark goes before, carried by priests. Christ goes before us through death but also goes with us through this life. Jordan is typical of Christ's death, not ours.

CHAPTER 5

*THEME:*Fear falls upon the Amorites; a new generation is circumcised; the divine visitor—captain of the
host

In this chapter we learn that the rite of circumcision was performed;
the manna ceased and they began to eat the old corn of the land;
finally, Joshua was confronted by the unseen Captain of the "host of
the Lord"—Joshua needed this vision at this time. These three things
are important to see.

FEAR FALLS UPON THE AMORITES

**And it came to pass, when all the kings of the Amorites,
which were on the side of Jordan westward, and all the
kings of the Canaanites, which were by the sea, heard
that the Lord had dried up the waters of Jordan from
before the children of Israel, until we were passed over,
that their heart melted, neither was there spirit in them
any more, because of the children of Israel [Josh. 5:1].**

Because the Jordan River was at flood stage, the Amorites and Canaanites did not expect the Israelites to cross over. They expected them
to cross over after the flood season was over. They probably thought
they had quite a bit more time to prepare for battle, and it was a shock
for them to discover that God had enabled Israel to cross Jordan.

A NEW GENERATION IS CIRCUMCISED

**At that time the Lord said unto Joshua, Make thee sharp
knives, and circumcise again the children of Israel the
second time.**

> And Joshua made him sharp knives, and circumcised the children of Israel at the hill of the foreskins.
>
> And this is the cause why Joshua did circumcise: All the people that came out of Egypt, that were males, even all the men of war, died in the wilderness by the way, after they came out of Egypt.
>
> Now all the people that came out were circumcised: but all the people that were born in the wilderness by the way as they came forth out of Egypt, them they had not circumcised [Josh. 5:2-5].

The new generation had neglected the rite of circumcision, which was the badge of the Abrahamic covenant. The Abrahamic covenant, you remember, gave Israel the land of Canaan. They had neglected to observe this rite during those years of wandering through the wilderness.

> For the children of Israel walked forty years in the wilderness, till all the people that were men of war, which came out of Egypt, were consumed, because they obeyed not the voice of the Lord: unto whom the Lord sware that he would not show them the land, which the Lord sware unto their fathers that he would give us, a land that floweth with milk and honey.
>
> And their children, whom he raised up in their stead, them Joshua circumcised: for they were uncircumcised, because they had not circumcised them by the way.
>
> And it came to pass, when they had done circumcising all the people, that they abode in their places in the camp, till they were whole.
>
> And the Lord said unto Joshua, This day have I rolled away the reproach of Egypt from off you. Wherefore the name of the place is called Gilgal unto this day [Josh. 5:6-9].

Both in spirit and in reality the children of Israel had not kept the rite of circumcision, which was the sign of the Abrahamic covenant. The children of Israel had walked forty years in the wilderness until all of the men that had come out of Egypt, who were men of war, had died. The Lord had given them children, and they are the ones whom Joshua circumcised. At this time, God rolled away the reproach of Egypt. The "reproach of Egypt" means that during the latter years of the Egyptian bondage this rite had been neglected, and the neglect had continued during the wilderness wanderings. Therefore, the place where Joshua circumcised the children of Israel was called *Gilgal*, which means "a rolling."

> **And the children of Israel encamped in Gilgal, and kept the passover on the fourteenth day of the month at even in the plains of Jericho [Josh. 5:10].**

It was in the spring of the year, at the time of the latter rains, that Israel performed the rite of circumcision and then celebrated the Passover. The reproach of Egypt was rolled away from Israel. God had promised to give the descendants of Abraham the land, and the promise was about to become a reality.

All of this has a spiritual message for us today. The old nature is no good. The old nature cannot inherit spiritual blessing. The old nature cannot even enjoy spiritual blessing. The old nature will not like Canaan, nor anything in the heavenlies. In Galatians 5:17 Paul says, "For the flesh lusteth [which is literally *wars*] against the Spirit, and the Spirit against the flesh: and these are contrary the one to the other: so that ye cannot do the things that ye would." Paul found that there was no good in the old nature. He also discovered that there was no power in the new nature (see Rom. 7). The circumcision of the children of Israel recognized these facts.

> **And they did eat of the old corn of the land on the morrow after the passover, unleavened cakes, and parched corn in the selfsame day.**

> And the manna ceased on the morrow after they had
> eaten of the old corn of the land; neither had the chil-
> dren of Israel manna any more; but they did eat of the
> fruit of the land of Canaan that year [Josh. 5:11–12].

Manna was a picture of Christ we are told in the New Testament. Jesus
said, "Your fathers did eat manna in the wilderness, and are dead.
This is the bread which cometh down from heaven, that a man may eat
thereof, and not die. I am the living bread which came down from
heaven: if any man eat of this bread, he shall live for ever: and the
bread that I will give is my flesh, which I will give for the life of the
world" (John 6:49–51). Manna represents Christ in His death. He is
the One who came down to this earth "to give his life a ransom for
many."

When Israel arrived in Canaan, the manna ceased, and they began
to eat the old corn of the land.

THE DIVINE VISITOR—CAPTAIN OF THE HOST

> And it came to pass, when Joshua was by Jericho, that
> he lifted up his eyes and looked, and, behold, there
> stood a man over against him with his sword drawn in
> his hand: and Joshua went unto him, and said unto him,
> Art thou for us, or for our adversaries?

> And he said, Nay; but as captain of the host of the LORD
> am I now come. And Joshua fell on his face to the earth,
> and did worship, and said unto him, What saith my
> lord unto his servant?

> And the captain of the LORD's host said unto Joshua,
> Loose thy shoe from off thy foot; for the place whereon
> thou standest is holy. And Joshua did so [Josh. 13–15].

This is the call and commission of Joshua. It is the same as Moses'
call on the plain of Midian at the burning bush. Moses was told to
remove his shoes, for the ground upon which he stood was holy (Exod.

3:5). The children of Israel had crossed the Jordan River and were camped on the other side. One morning Joshua probably got up and looked over the scene. It was an impressive sight. There were the camps of all twelve tribes of Israel around him. As he looked at it, I think he swelled with a little pride. He was the one in charge, and GHQ was in his tent now. Then he happened to look down at the edge of the camp, and he saw someone with a drawn sword. Joshua may have thought, *There is someone down there who doesn't seem to know that I am the general here. I'd better go down there and put that fellow in his place!* So he walked down there and, according to our translation, said, "Art thou for us, or for our adversaries?" Now in good old Americana he said, "What's the big idea? Who gave you an order to draw a sword?" Then that One, whom I believe was the pre-incarnate Christ, turned to him, and when He turned, He said, "Nay; but as captain of the host of the LORD am I now come!" Notice the reaction of Joshua. He fell on his face before Him.

You see, Joshua learned that GHQ was not in his tent after all. It was at the throne of God. *God* was leading them. Actually, he was not captain of the hosts of the Lord; he was under Someone else. And he would be taking orders from Him. We shall be seeing this in the next chapter as he marches the army around the city of Jericho for seven straight days. If you had stopped Joshua on the sixth day and said, "Look, General Joshua, this is a silly thing to be doing," he probably would have said, "That's exactly what I think." "Then why are you doing it? You are in command here." Joshua would say, "You are wrong. I take my orders from Someone above me. I am only a buck private in the rear ranks. I am doing this because I have been commanded to do it."

CHAPTER 6

THEME: Conquest of Jericho

Now that we have come to the actual conquest of the Promised Land, let's look again at the events that led up to it.

The children of Israel have now crossed the Jordan River in a most remarkable manner, and they have entered the land. The Jordan is a quiet little stream in the summertime, but it is a rushing torrent during the rainy seasons. As you recall, the ark of the Lord, carried by the priests, went before them. The ark, of course, represents the presence of Christ. When the feet of the priests reached the Jordan, the waters rolled back; then they stood in the midst of the river, with the ark on their shoulders, while all the people passed over Jordan and the memorial stones were set up.

Now the people of Israel are camped on the west side of the bank of the Jordan River. What a glorious, wonderful anticipation awaits them! This is the land God had promised to give them, a land of milk and honey. It is the land they have been told to possess. Obviously, their hearts are thrilled with it. Surges of anticipation and joy go through them.

They have been conditioned for conquest by circumcision, which was the token of the covenant God made with Abraham. Part of that covenant was that they were to have that land. You recall that Joshua made sharp knives for the circumcision.

What application does this have to your life and mine? To me the sharp knives speak of the Word of God, which ". . . is quick, and powerful, and sharper than any two-edged sword . . ." (Heb. 4:12). It is able to divide. In our country today all the morality lines are rubbed out, but there is still black and white in the Word of God. We need to get back to Bible morality, because there is no blessing to this nation or any people until they come back to the Word of God.

Another conditioning for conquest had been the vision of the Cap-

tain of the hosts of the Lord. General Joshua is going to take orders
from above.

Now the first step of conquest is Jericho, and we see that the tactic
is to divide the land. By taking the cities of Jericho and Ai, the center of
the land will be theirs; then they will move into the south. This
method of dividing the land is a method that was followed, it seems,
by great generals from that day to this. They divide the enemy, then
take them piecemeal. It was used in the Civil War, in World War I, and
in World War II. However, the *method* for taking Jericho would not be
used again. Let's look at it.

> Now Jericho was straitly shut up because of the children
> of Israel: none went out, and none came in [Josh. 6:1].

Jericho was prepared for the attack of the Israelites. They did not think
the Israelites would arrive as quickly as they did, but they shut up the
city and prepared for attack.

> And the LORD said unto Joshua, See, I have given into
> thine hand Jericho, and the king thereof, and the mighty
> men of valour.
>
> And ye shall compass the city, all ye men of war, and go
> round about the city once. Thus shalt thou do six days.
>
> And seven priests shall bear before the ark seven trum-
> pets of rams' horns: and the seventh day ye shall com-
> pass the city seven times, and the priests shall blow with
> the trumpets.
>
> And it shall come to pass, that when they make a long
> blast with the ram's horn, and when ye hear the sound
> of the trumpet, all the people shall shout with a great
> shout; and the wall of the city shall fall down flat, and
> the people shall ascend up every man straight before
> him [Josh. 6:2–5].

The day comes for the beginning of the campaign. Joshua follows the Lord's instructions exactly.

> And it came to pass, when Joshua had spoken unto the people, that the seven priests bearing the seven trumpets of rams' horns passed on before the LORD, and blew with the trumpets: and the ark of the covenant of the LORD followed them.
>
> And the armed men went before the priests that blew with the trumpets, and the rereward came after the ark, the priests going on, and blowing with the trumpets.
>
> And Joshua had commanded the people, saying, Ye shall not shout, nor make any noise with your voice, neither shall any word proceed out of your mouth, until the day I bid you shout; then shall ye shout.
>
> So the ark of the LORD compassed the city, going about it once: and they came into the camp, and lodged in the camp [Josh. 6:8–11].

The city of Jericho is prepared. Undoubtedly there are soldiers on the wall and watchmen at the gate. The military brass and its staff are in the city getting reports from the wall. Finally the word comes, "Here comes the enemy." Joshua and the army of Israel are marching toward the city. In front of the procession is the ark carried by the priests, and the priests carry horns. A watchman on the wall cries, "Here they come. Let's get ready. They apparently are going to attack at the gate!" So the forces of Jericho gather at the gate. They are ready for battle if the gate is broken down.

Then a strange thing happens. The watchman calls down, "They're not going to attack here. They made a turn and they are going to attack at another place!" So the army on the inside shifts, and I think they march around on the inside. They are informed by those on the wall, "They are here . . . they are here . . . they are here." The Israelites go all the way around, and instead of attacking, they go back into

camp! You can be sure of one thing: there is a huddle that night of the
king and the military brass.

> **And Joshua rose early in the morning, and the priests
> took up the ark of the LORD.**

> **And seven priests bearing seven trumpets of rams'
> horns before the ark of the LORD went on continually,
> and blew with the trumpets: and the armed men went
> before them; but the rereward came after the ark of the
> LORD, the priests going on, and blowing with the trum-
> pets.**

> **And the second day they compassed the city once, and
> returned into the camp: so they did six days [Josh.
> 6:12–14].**

The next day the Israelites give a repeat performance. The watchman
on the wall cries out, "Here they come again." Then the Israelites
march around the wall and go back to camp. Each day for six days they
do the same thing. By the sixth day, the midnight oil had burned long
and late in the Pentagon inside Jericho. The army on the outside was
tired of marching around the wall. Maybe some of the children of Israel were saying, "What we are doing looks foolish!" If you had asked
Joshua why he was doing this, he probably would have replied, "I take
my orders from the captain of the hosts of the Lord. This is what He
has told me to do and I am doing it."

> **And it came to pass on the seventh day, that they rose
> early about the dawning of the day, and compassed the
> city after the same manner seven times: only on that day
> they compassed the city seven times [Josh. 6:15].**

So on the seventh day the Israelites march around the wall again. The
people of Jericho heave a sigh of relief when they get clear around. The
army inside the wall has made its circuit, too, and is relieved that it is
over for the day. Everyone sits down to rest—when all of a sudden the

watchman says, "Wait a minute, they are going to march around again." So the Israelites make the circuit again. They do it a third and a fourth time. . . .

And it came to pass at the seventh time, when the priests blew with the trumpets, Joshua said unto the people, Shout; for the LORD hath given you the city.

So the people shouted when the priests blew with the trumpets: and it came to pass, when the people heard the sound of the trumpet, and the people shouted with a great shout, that the wall fell down flat, so that the people went up into the city, every man straight before him, and they took the city [Josh. 6:16, 20].

The walls of Jericho fell down flat. I had the privilege of going to Jericho with a very special Arab guide who had worked with both John Garstang and Kathleen Kenyon; they had led archaeological expeditions in unearthing the ancient city of Jericho. Garstang and Kenyon disagreed as to the dates of the wall. But it had fallen down and was flat—that was obvious. Since this Arab guide had worked with both expeditions, I asked him what he thought as to the date of ancient Jericho. He went along with Garstang, and his reasoning was that when Garstang got there, he was probably not as scientific and didn't do quite the job that Kenyon did. Because he disturbed everything, it would be impossible for anyone coming later to arrive at an accurate estimation. Well, I'll let them argue that. All I'm interested in is that the Word of God says the walls fell down flat—and the evidence is there today. The faith of the believer does not rest upon the shovel of the archaeologist. "By faith the walls of Jericho fell down, after they were compassed about seven days" (Heb. 11:30).

Jericho represents the *world* to the believer. It is strong and formidable and foreboding—the conquest depends upon faith: "For whatsoever is born of God overcometh the world: and this is the victory that overcometh the world, even our faith" (1 John 5:4). Hebrews 11 reveals how faith worked in all ages in the lives of God's choicest servants as they met the world head-on and overcame by faith.

We hear the song, "Joshua Fit the Battle of Jericho." The question is—did he? No, he did not. He didn't fight at all. He just marched around the city. Who did the fighting? God did that, friend, and I think any other explanation is ridiculous. Some say that an earthquake took place at that psychological moment when the priests blew the trumpets and all the people shouted, and the shock toppled the walls. Others say that the constant marching of the children of Israel around the wall loosened the wall and it fell down. Well, you can believe that if you want to. I like it the way it is told in the Word of God. God got the victory; Israel got the possession.

A great problem that many believers have today is that they are trying to "fit the battle of Jericho" and overcome the world. But you and I need to start taking orders from the Captain up yonder, the Captain of our salvation.

Now notice two more things briefly. The first is that Rahab was spared.

> But Joshua had said unto the two men that had spied out the country, Go into the harlot's house, and bring out thence the woman, and all that she hath, as ye sware unto her.
>
> And the young men that were spies went in, and brought out Rahab, and her father, and her mother, and her brethren, and all that she had; and they brought out all her kindred, and left them without the camp of Israel.
>
> And Joshua saved Rahab the harlot alive, and her father's household, and all that she had; and she dwelleth in Israel even unto this day; because she hid the messengers, which Joshua sent to spy out Jericho [Josh. 6:22–23, 25].

True to their promise, they saved Rahab and all her family that was with her in the house.

Note also that Joshua pronounced a curse on anyone who would rebuild that city.

**And Joshua adjured them at that time, saying, Cursed
be the man before the LORD, that riseth up and buildeth
this city Jericho: he shall lay the foundation thereof in
his firstborn, and in his youngest son shall he set up the
gates of it [Josh. 6:26].**

We will see when we study 1 Kings 16 that Jericho was rebuilt. And
the curse came upon the man who rebuilt it and upon his son.

Before we leave this chapter, notice the explicit command of God,
as relayed by Joshua, was that nothing was to be salvaged in the city
but the silver, gold, and vessels of bronze and iron, which were to be
placed in the treasury of the Lord. No soldier was to take anything for
himself.

**And ye, in any wise keep yourselves from the accursed
thing, lest ye make yourselves accursed, when ye take of
the accursed thing, and make the camp of Israel a
curse, and trouble it [Josh. 6:18].**

We will see in the next chapter that somebody snitched at the battle of
Jericho.

CHAPTER 7

THEME: Defeat at Ai

The worst enemy that you have is yourself. He occupies the same skin that you occupy. He uses the same brain that you use in thinking his destructive thoughts. He uses the same hands that you use to perform his own deeds. This enemy can do you more harm than anyone else. He is the greatest handicap that you have in your daily Christian life.

There are two factors that make dealing with this enemy doubly difficult. In the first place, we are reluctant to recognize and identify him. We are loath to label him as an enemy. The fact of the matter is most of us rather like him. The second problem is that he is on the inside of us. If he would only come out and fight like a man, it would be different, but he will not. It is not because he is a coward, but because he can fight better from his position within.

Nations, cities, churches, and individuals have been destroyed by the enemy within. Russia fell to the Communists, not because of the German pressure on the outside, but because of this doctrine fomenting on the inside.

There comes out of ancient history an authentic narrative, long held in the category of mythology, that the city of Troy held off the Greeks for ten long, weary years. Finally the Greeks sailed away leaving a wooden horse. The Trojans took that wooden horse within their gates, and that was the undoing and destruction of Troy.

In a similar way churches are wrecked from within, not from forces without. The Lord Jesus Christ, in letters to the seven churches in Asia Minor, gave them certain warnings; yet not one of these churches received warning as to the enemy on the outside. He said: ". . . Thou hast there some that hold the teaching of Balaam. . . . So that thou also some that hold the teaching of the Nicolaitans in like manner" (Rev. 2:14–15 ASV). Also He warned: "But I have this against thee, that thou sufferest the woman Jezebel, who calleth herself a prophetess; and she teacheth and seduceth my servants to commit fornication, and to eat things sacrificed to idols" (Rev. 2:20 ASV). Christ said to these churches (in effect), "You have something within that is bringing about your own destruction." Disloyalty and unfaithfulness in the church today is hurting God's cause more than any enemy that is on the outside. The devil can only hurt our churches from the inside, not from the outside.

Also, my friend, an individual can be destroyed from the inside. Alexander the Great was probably the greatest military genius who has moved armies across the pages of history. There has been no one like him. Before the age of thirty-five he had conquered the world, but he died a drunkard. He had conquered the world, but he could not conquer Alexander the Great. There was an enemy within that destroyed him.

The only battle that the children of Israel lost in taking the Promised Land was a battle in which the defeat came, not from without, but from within. When the children of Israel entered the Promised Land, not many enemies, but three conspicuous and outstanding ones stood in their way. They were Jericho, Ai, and the Gibeonites. These three enemies of Israel prevented Israel's enjoyment and possession of the Promised Land. The land was there. God had told them that it was theirs. God had given them the title deed in His promise to Abraham. To Joshua He had said, "Every place that the sole of your foot shall tread upon, to you have I given it, as I spake unto Moses" (Josh. 1:3 ASV). God was saying to them, "It is yours, go in, possess, and enjoy that which you take."

What a lesson that is for us today. These people were given a land that was made up of three hundred thousand square miles, and even in their best days they only occupied thirty thousand square miles. Christians have been given all spiritual blessings. But how many of them, Christian, are you enjoying today? How many of them are really yours? You have the title to them, but have you claimed them and are you enjoying them as He intended? Think of the many Christians who are blessed with all spiritual blessings and yet are living as if they are spiritual paupers. God has made them available to us but, if we are to get them, there are battles to be fought and victories to be won. In fact, the Epistle to the Ephesians closes with the clanking of armor and the sound of battle, with the call to put on the whole armor of God.

In Joshua 7 and 8, defeat and victory at Ai represent the flesh in the believer. The sin of Achan was sin in the camp. Steps in sins of flesh are: I saw—physical; I coveted—mental; I took—volitional. There will be no deliverance until sin is dealt with in the life of a believer.

Now let us look at the text.

> **But the children of Israel committed a trespass in the accursed thing: for Achan, the son of Carmi, the son of Zabdi, the son of Zerah, of the tribe of Judah, took of the accursed thing: and the anger of the LORD was kindled against the children of Israel [Josh. 7:1].**

This verse tells us that the children of Israel committed a trespass, but it was one man, Achan, who committed the sin. The whole nation had to suffer because of what Achan did. This is interesting because many people stand on the outside and criticize the church. They talk about the failure of the church and its apostasy. I do some of this myself. But, my friend, talking about the church as a member is one thing, and standing on the outside doing nothing is quite another. If the church is failing and is in a state of apostasy (and it is), then you and I are implicated in it as members of the church. If one member suffers, then all members suffer. "And whether one member suffer, all the members suffer with it; or one member be honoured, all the members rejoice with it" (1 Cor. 12:26).

> **And Joshua sent men from Jericho to Ai, which is beside Beth-aven, on the east side of Beth-el, and spake unto them, saying, Go up and view the country. And the men went up and viewed Ai.**

> **And they returned to Joshua, and said unto him, Let not all the people go up; but let about two or three thousand men go up and smite Ai; and make not all the people to labour thither; for they are but few [Josh. 7:2–3].**

Jericho represented the world; Ai represents the flesh. Some saints are marching around Jericho, blowing trumpets as they talk about being separated Christians. But they are as negative as anyone could be as they declare, "We don't do this, and we don't do that." In fact, they do a spiritual strip-tease—they put off everything that seems to them to be worldly. They have overcome the world. But what about the flesh, friends? Some of the most dangerous people in the church are the super-duper saints who talk about having overcome the world, but they are defeated at Ai. Some of them have the meanest tongues imaginable. I was a pastor for forty years, and I could tell you story after story about the antics of the super-duper saints. The flesh has many people in tow. They think they are living the Christian life. In fact, they talk about living the victorious life, yet they do not even know what it is. The victorious life is *His* life. He is the One who gets the victory and not us.

The children of Israel were in the flush of victory. They had overcome Jericho. Although it was God's victory, in a short time Israel thought of it as their victory. Joshua sent some of his men to look at Ai. After looking the city over carefully, they said, "Ai is nothing compared to Jericho." When I was in that land, I looked at it through binoculars—we didn't even go up to it. It is a little old place and doesn't amount to much.

> So there went up thither of the people about three thousand men: and they fled before the men of Ai.
>
> And the men of Ai smote of them about thirty and six men: for they chased them from before the gate even unto Shebarim, and smote them in the going down: wherefore the hearts of the people melted, and became as water [Josh. 7:4–5].

Israel was defeated by the men of Ai. You and I are defeated by the flesh. We cannot use the same tactics to overcome the flesh as we use to overcome the world. The Israelites did not recognize their weakness. The apostle Paul recognized his weakness when he said, "For I know that in me (that is, in my flesh,) dwelleth no good thing: for to will is present with me; but how to perform that which is good I find not" (Rom. 7:18). Have you found out, my Christian friend, that you have no strength or power within yourself? You cannot live the Christian life, and God never asks you to. God wants to live the Christian life through you. In Romans 7 Paul discovered that there was no good thing in his old nature. He also found out that there was no power in his new nature. The new nature wants to live for God but does not have the power to do it. In Romans 8 we are introduced to the Holy Spirit of God. It is only when we are filled with the Holy Spirit of God that we can live the Christian life.

> **And Joshua rent his clothes, and fell to the earth upon his face before the ark of the LORD until the eventide, he and the elders of Israel, and put dust upon their heads.**

> **And Joshua said, Alas, O Lord GOD, wherefore hast thou at all brought this people over Jordan, to deliver us into the hand of the Amorites, to destroy us? would to God we had been content, and dwelt on the other side Jordan! [Josh. 7:6–7].**

We have heard this song before. Joshua is singing the blues. He learned the lyrics in the wilderness with the children of Israel. Joshua did not sing this song in the wilderness, but he is singing now. He cannot understand why he lost the battle. So he tears his clothes and cries out:

> **O Lord, what shall I say, when Israel turneth their backs before their enemies!**

> **For the Canaanites and all the inhabitants of the land shall hear of it, and shall environ us round, and cut off our name from the earth: and what wilt thou do unto thy great name? [Josh. 7:8–9].**

Listen to what the Lord said. It is getting right down to the nitty-gritty.

> **And the LORD said unto Joshua, Get thee up; wherefore liest thou thus upon thy face? [Josh. 7:10].**

He says to Joshua, "Get up off your face, and cut out all this whining in sackcloth and ashes." There are Christians who spend their prayer time whining before the Lord. It won't do any good, friend. We need to get at the root of the problem.

> **Israel hath sinned, and they have also transgressed my covenant which I commanded them: for they have even taken of the accursed thing, and have also stolen, and dissembled also, and they have put it even among their own stuff [Josh. 7:11].**

Joshua did not know that Israel had sinned. He did not have the spiritual discernment that was in the early church. When Ananias and Sapphira lied about their property in Acts 5, the Holy Spirit brought it out immediately. The early church was sensitive to sin.

God told Joshua that sin was in the camp and he would have to deal with it.

> **In the morning therefore ye shall be brought according to your tribes: and it shall be, that the tribe which the LORD taketh shall come according to the families thereof; and the family which the LORD shall take shall come by households; and the household which the LORD shall take shall come man by man [Josh. 7:14].**

The tribe of Judah and the family of the Zarhites were found to be guilty.

> **And he brought his household man by man; and Achan, the son of Carmi, the son of Zabdi, the son of Zerah, of the tribe of Judah, was taken [Josh. 7:18].**

Israel had to go through this long procedure in order to find the guilty party. It was difficult for them to distinguish evil in the camp. For us, also, it seems to be difficult to distinguish evil in the church. Church members seem to be the most blind to evil in their own communities. They can see evil in a night club downtown or in a liquor store or in some politician, but they cannot see sin in their family or church. How tragic that is.

> **And Joshua said unto Achan, My son, give, I pray thee, glory to the LORD God of Israel, and make confession unto him; and tell me now what thou hast done; hide it not from me.**
>
> **And Achan answered Joshua, and said, Indeed I have sinned against the LORD God of Israel, and thus and thus have I done:**
>
> **When I saw among the spoils a goodly Babylonish garment, and two hundred shekels of silver, and a wedge of gold of fifty shekels weight, then I coveted them, and took them; and, behold, they are hid in the earth in the midst of my tent, and the silver under it [Josh. 7:19–21].**

Notice the steps of Achan's sin. He saw, he coveted, he took. These are the steps of the sin of the flesh. Gossip, criticism, envy, and jealousy are all sins of the flesh. They cause strife and trouble. For instance, criticism builds up your ego. It calls attention to yourself. It makes you look better than the person you are criticizing. The old sin of the flesh sees, covets, and then takes.

Now what does Achan do when he is confronted? He confesses. He lays it right out. For believers today, how are we going to overcome the flesh? We have to deal with sin in our lives.

You remember that the way we overcome the world is by faith. But that isn't the way we overcome the flesh. We want to have fellowship with God; we want to be filled by the Holy Spirit that we might serve Him. Now how are we going to have fellowship with Him? How are we going to have power in our lives? John's first epistle makes it clear the way we *can't* do it: ". . . God is light, and in him is no darkness at all. If we say that we have fellowship with him, and walk in darkness, we lie, and do not the truth" (1 John 1:5–6). If you say you are having fellowship with Him and are living in sin, you are not kidding anybody. You certainly are not having fellowship with Him, and you know it. Now suppose we say we have no sin. "If we say that we have no sin, we deceive ourselves, and the truth is not in us" (1 John 1:8). But what are we to do? "If we confess our sins, he is faithful and just to forgive us our sins, and to cleanse us from all unrighteousness" (1 John 1:9). You see, you cannot bring God down to your level. And friend, you cannot bring yourself up to God's level. The thing to do is to keep the communication open between you and God. And the only way you can do it is by confessing your sin. John adds, "If we say that we have not sinned, we make him a liar, and his word is not in us" (1 John 1:10). That is strong language, friend. God says if we say we have no sin we are lying. And I believe He is accurate. But what do we do about it? We are to confess our sins.

How are we to do that? True confession does not deal in generalities. Spell it out as Achan did: "I saw them; I coveted them; I took them." Tell God everything that is in your heart—just open it up to Him. You might as well tell Him because He already knows all about it.

Mel Trotter told about a man on the board of his Pacific Garden Mission, a doctor, who, when he prayed would say, "Lord, if I have sinned, forgive my sins." Mel Trotter got tired of listening to that. Finally he went to the doctor and said to him, "Listen, Doc, you say, 'If I have sinned.' Don't you know whether or not you have sinned?" The doctor said, "Well, I guess I do." "Don't you know what your sin is?" "No," the doctor said, "I don't know what it is." Mel Trotter said, "If you don't know, then guess at it!" The next time the doctor prayed, Mel said, he guessed it the first time! It is amazing, friends, the way we beat around the bush even in our praying. Just go to God and tell Him exactly what your sin is. That is confession. There can be no joy in your life; there can be no power in your life; there can be no victory in your life until there is confession of sin.

And Joshua said, Why hast thou troubled us? the Lord
shall trouble thee this day. And all Israel stoned him

> with stones, and burned them with fire, after they had
> stoned them with stones.
>
> And they raised over him a great heap of stones unto
> this day. So the LORD turned from the fierceness of his
> anger. Wherefore the name of that place was called, The
> valley of Achor, unto this day [Josh. 7:25–26].

This is a serious situation, and it is emphasized for believers in the
New Testament. "For if ye live after the flesh, ye shall die: but if ye
through the Spirit do mortify the deeds of the body, ye shall live"
(Rom. 8:13). There are many Christians who are not living. Dwight L.
Moody put it in this quaint way, "People have just enough religion to
make them miserable." There are miserable saints because they do not
deal with the sin in their lives. The apostle Paul said, "For if we would
judge ourselves, we should not be judged. But when we are judged,
we are chastened of the Lord, that we should not be condemned with
the world" (1 Cor. 11:31–32). If we don't judge ourselves, God has to
step in and judge us, and His judgment is sometimes pretty serious. I
can tell you from experience what the judgment of God is in my own
life. And it will do no good to complain and whine like Joshua did.
The thing to do is to go to God and get the miserable thing straight-
ened out. When we confess our sin to Him and turn from it, then we
experience the joy of the Lord.

CHAPTER 8

THEME: Victory at Ai; Joshua reads the blessings and cursings

A s we have seen in chapter 7, Israel suffered an ignoble defeat at the little city of Ai, and the reason for the defeat was sin in the camp. Now the sin has been dealt with, and God is prepared to give Israel the victory.

VICTORY AT AI

And the Lord said unto Joshua, Fear not, neither be thou dismayed: take all the people of war with thee, and arise, go up to Ai: see, I have given into thy hand the king of Ai, and his people, and his city, and his land [Josh. 8:1].

Notice that God says to take *all* the men of war when they go against Ai. As we have said, Ai represents the flesh. The flesh is the greatest enemy you have, and you need all the resources you have to get the victory.

And thou shalt do to Ai and her king as thou didst unto Jericho and her king: only the spoil thereof, and the cattle thereof, shall ye take for a prey unto yourselves: lay thee an ambush for the city behind it [Josh. 8:2].

You will recall that at the battle of Jericho they were not to take any of the prey or the spoil for themselves. But here God tells them to take what they want. Why the difference? Well, we now know that in Jericho social diseases were running rampant. Joshua didn't know about disease germs, but God did.

Note that God tells Joshua to take Ai by ambush.

So Joshua arose, and all the people of war, to go up against Ai: and Joshua chose out thirty thousand mighty men of valour, and sent them away by night.

And he commanded them, saying, Behold, ye shall lie in wait against the city, even behind the city: go not very far from the city, but be ye all ready:

And I, and all the people that are with me, will approach unto the city: and it shall come to pass, when they come out against us, as at the first, that we will flee before them,

(For they will come out after us) till we have drawn them from the city; for they will say, They flee before us, as at the first: therefore we will flee before them.

Then ye shall rise up from the ambush, and seize upon the city: for the LORD your God will deliver it into your hand [Josh. 8:3-7].

As we read on, we see that the strategy worked just as Joshua planned, and the city of Ai fell easily into the hands of Israel.

Because Ai represents the flesh, we learn from this episode great spiritual lessons. First of all there must be a recognition of the enemy and his potential. We must realize that the greatest enemy you and I have is ourselves. I hear folk saying, "The devil made me do it." Well, he didn't. It is that flesh of yours which is responsible.

Second, we must examine very carefully the reasons for our defeats. Primarily the reason for defeat is our dependence upon our own ability. You remember that the spies said to Joshua, "You will need only about two or three thousand men to overcome little Ai." And we think the flesh will be easy to overcome. We depend on ourselves to do it. We will have to come to the same place to which Paul came when he cried, "O wretched man that I am! who shall deliver me from the body of this death?" (Rom. 7:24).

My friend, you and I cannot control the flesh. Only the Spirit of God can do that. The tragedy is that thousands are trying to control and eradicate it in their own strength. You might as well take a gallon of French perfume out to the barnyard, pour it on a pile of manure, and expect to make it into a sand pile in which your children might play. You cannot improve and control this thing we know as the flesh or the sin nature. God says you cannot. Only the Holy Spirit can control it.

Christ died not only that you might have salvation, but He died that this sin nature might be dealt with. ". . . God sending his own Son in the likeness of sinful flesh, and for sin, condemned sin in the flesh" (Rom. 8:3). This simply means that when Christ came to this earth, He not only died for your sins that you might have salvation, but He died to bring into judgment this old sin nature. Otherwise God could not touch us with a forty-foot pole, because we are evil. Christ died because I have a sin nature and you have a sin nature. The Holy Spirit could not touch us until Christ had paid that penalty. When the penalty was paid, and our sin nature was condemned, then the Holy Spirit could and did come into our lives and bring victory out of defeat. As Paul expressed it, "I am crucified with Christ: nevertheless I live; yet not I, but Christ liveth in me: and the life which I now live in the flesh I live by the faith of the Son of God, who loved me, and gave himself for me" (Gal. 2:20). The flesh, like Ai, will defeat us unless we are depending upon the power of the Holy Spirit to win the victory.

JOSHUA READS THE BLESSINGS AND CURSINGS

Then Joshua built an altar unto the Lord God of Israel in mount Ebal,

As Moses the servant of the Lord commanded the children of Israel, as it is written in the book of the law of Moses, an altar of whole stones, over which no man hath lift up any iron: and they offered thereon burnt offerings unto the Lord, and sacrificed peace offerings.

And he wrote there upon the stones a copy of the law of Moses, which he wrote in the presence of the children of Israel [Josh. 8:30–32].

We find that after the victory at Ai, Joshua built an altar unto the Lord God of Israel in Mount Ebal. Then the Israelites did what Moses had commanded, and Joshua read the blessings and cursings (see Deut. 11:26–32).

> **And afterward he read all the words of the law, the blessings and cursings, according to all that is written in the book of the law.**
>
> **There was not a word of all that Moses commanded, which Joshua read not before all the congregation of Israel, with the women, and the little ones, and the strangers that were conversant among them [Josh. 8:34–35].**

Note that the entire Law of Moses was read. They did not read just a part of it; they read all of it. This was to be the law of the land, and it was time for Israel to be reminded of the conditions of God's covenant with her.

CHAPTER 9

THEME: Compact with the Gibeonites

As Joshua began the conquest of the Promised Land, he faced three formidable enemies: Jericho, Ai, and the Gibeonites. These three enemies of Joshua represent the enemies of the Christian today. Jericho represents the *world*; Ai represents the *flesh*; and the Gibeonites represent the *devil*.

You will recall that Joshua's strategy was to first take Jericho, located right in the center of the land, then to take Ai which stood northeast of Jericho. To the south was an alliance of Gibeonites. Apparently they were next in the line of conquest. But the Gibeonites were clever, as we shall see.

> **And it came to pass, when all the kings which were on this side Jordan, in the hills, and in the valleys, and in all the coasts of the great sea over against Lebanon, the Hittite, and the Amorite, the Canaanite, the Perizzite, the Hivite, and the Jebusite, heard thereof;**

> **That they gathered themselves together, to fight with Joshua and with Israel, with one accord [Josh. 9:1–2].**

Undoubtedly these kings had planned to unite against the Israelites, but it seems that for some reason they failed to come together, and they did not succeed in stopping the invading army of Israel. This may explain the defection of the Gibeonites. Their thought was not to fight but to make a compact.

> **And when the inhabitants of Gibeon heard what Joshua had done unto Jericho and to Ai,**

> **They did work wilily, and went and made as if they had been ambassadors, and took old sacks upon their asses, and wine bottles, old, and rent, and bound up;**

And old shoes and clouted upon their feet, and old garments upon them; and all the bread of their provision
was dry and mouldy.

And they went to Joshua unto the camp at Gilgal, and
said unto him, and to the men of Israel, We be come
from a far country: now therefore make ye a league with
us.

And the men of Israel said unto the Hivites, Peradven-
ture ye dwell among us; and how shall we make a
league with you?

And they said unto Joshua, We are thy servants. And
Joshua said unto them, Who are ye? and from whence
come ye?

And they said unto him, From a very far country thy
servants are come because of the name of the LORD thy
God: for we have heard the fame of him, and all that he
did in Egypt [Josh. 9:3–9].

The Gibeonites were very clever, and they were a bunch of liars. They
pretended to be envoys from a far country when, in fact, they lived
only a few miles from Jerusalem. They told Joshua that they really
wanted to worship the living and true God. Then they called Joshua's
attention—if it hadn't been noticed—to their old sacks and wineskins,
their old shoes and threadbare clothing, and their moldy bread. It was
all a hoax, but Joshua fell for it. God had ordered the Israelites to completely wipe out the people of the land and to make no treaties with
them. Although it was Joshua's intent to obey God, he was deceived
into making peace with the Gibeonites and actually making a league
with them. Notice that neither Joshua nor the men of Israel asked the
mind of God before entering into this alliance.

As you recall, Jericho represents the world. How do you overcome
the world? By faith. Ai represents the flesh. How do you overcome the
flesh? Not by fighting it, but by recognizing your weakness, confess-

ing to God, and letting the Spirit of God get the victory. Remember that it was God who said, "I'm going to give you Ai."

Now we have the third enemy, the Gibeonites, who represent for us the devil. Since Ephesians in the New Testament corresponds to the Book of Joshua in the Old Testament, we find an important parallel here. "Put on the whole armor of God, that ye may be able to stand against the wiles of the devil" (Eph. 6:11). As the men of Israel should have been beware of the wiles of the Gibeonites, so the believer today should watch for the wiles of the devil. "For we wrestle not against flesh and blood, but against principalities, against powers, against the rulers of the darkness of this world, against spiritual wickedness in high places" (Eph. 6:12). Our real enemy today is not a flesh and blood enemy, but a spiritual enemy. He is Satan. Yet how many Christians even recognize him today? What does he do? He tries to trick you into following him. I am not sure that he is interested in making a drunkard or a drug addict out of you. I think he is ashamed of that crowd of his in the bars and in the sinful places of the world. He went to church last Sunday, and he will be there next Sunday. He wants to be religious, and he wants you to fall down and worship him. He is clever and many Christians are taken in by him. The devil can pull the wool over our eyes. In 2 Corinthians 2:11 Paul says, "Lest Satan should get an advantage of us: for we are not ignorant of his devices." Unfortunately, you and I are sometimes ignorant of his devices.

Now how do we overcome this enemy? James 4:7 says, "Submit yourselves therefore to God. Resist the devil, and he will flee from you." My friend, we need to submit ourselves to God—that's the first thing. Oh, how we need to stay close to Him in this day in which we live! Satan is out to deceive us as believers. He works wilily. Frankly, I am amazed at the stupidity of the saints today. They are taken in by every ruse imaginable. Do you know why religious rackets are flourishing? It is because Christians are supporting them without doing any investigation. We need to resist the devil. We are to have nothing to do with that about which we are not well informed. There is danger of being linked up with him today, just as the men of Israel in their naiveté became linked up with the Gibeonites.

When Israel discovered that the Gibeonites were neighbors, and had tricked them, they still honored the treaty they had made with them.

> But all the princes said unto all the congregation, We have sworn unto them by the LORD God of Israel: now therefore we may not touch them.
>
> This we will do to them; we will even let them live, lest wrath be upon us, because of the oath which we sware unto them [Josh. 9:19–20].

The treaty was honored in that day, although made under these circumstances. Now you may think these folk back here in the Old Testament were uncivilized, but notice that a man's word was very important. And that is the way God wants it today.

> And the princes said unto them, Let them live; but let them be hewers of wood and drawers of water unto all the congregation; as the princes had promised them.
>
> And Joshua made them that day hewers of wood and drawers of water for the congregation, and for the altar of the LORD, even unto this day, in the place which he should choose [Josh. 9:21, 27].

CHAPTER 10

THEME: Southern campaign: five kings conquered;
the sun stood still

In this chapter Joshua conquers five kings of the Amorites, as he continues the campaign in the south. He completes the campaign in the south by the destruction of Makkedah, Lachish, Libnah, Eglon, Hebron, and Debir.

This chapter contains the account of the long day of Joshua. "Did Joshua make the sun stand still?" is a question which is asked by skeptic and saint alike. Following are some explanations of the long day of Joshua which have been proposed:

1. It is the practice of some to avoid giving any interpretation. They ignore it entirely as if it were not worthy of comment.

2. Some treat the language as poetic (v. 12). This is to adopt a nonliteral interpretation which dismisses the miraculous from the incident entirely. Those who hold to this view generally refer to Judges 5:20, ". . . the stars in their courses fought against Sisera." I refuse to dismiss this as poetic because we do not have enough information to state dogmatically that these are poetic statements and not matters of fact. It reminds us of the old bromide that poetic language is sometimes prosaic lying.

3. Some call this a miracle of refraction. The emphasis is placed on verse 13.

4. Some adopt the position that God stopped the entire solar system. They make Joshua's day 23 hours and 20 minutes. The other 40 minutes is found in 2 Kings 20:8–11, where the sun went ten degrees backward for a sign to Hezekiah that his life would be extended.

5. Some adopt the position that God blacked out the sun rather than continued its shining. The Berkeley Version translates it, "O Sun, wait in Gibeon." In the ASV the marginal reading is, "Sun, be silent." Maunder in the International Standard Bible Encyclopedia takes this position. Joshua had made a forced march all night (about forty miles),

attacked the enemy from the rear—came suddenly upon them. It was July—about 105° or 120° in the shade, and there was no shade. Joshua did not want more sun—he wanted less sun.

6. The best explanation, it seems, is a combination of numbers 4 and 5. Joshua needed more light and less heat. God covered the sun with a storm of hailstones. God slowed down the earth (v. 12). "Upon Gibeon" indicates that the sun was directly over—bisecting Gibeon— and the moon was going down "in the valley of Ajalon." Gibeon is latitude 31 degrees, 51 minutes north.

This is a miracle.

THE MIRACULOUS DEFENSE OF GIBEON

The background for all the action in this chapter is the treaty Joshua made with the Gibeonites. Of course, he should not have made this treaty, but since he did, he felt bound to it.

> Now it came to pass, when Adoni-zedek king of Jerusalem had heard how Joshua had taken Ai, and had utterly destroyed it; as he had done to Jericho and her king, so he had done to Ai and her king; and how the inhabitants of Gibeon had made peace with Israel, and were among them;

> That they feared greatly, because Gibeon was a great city, as one of the royal cities, and because it was greater than Ai, and all the men thereof were mighty.

> Wherefore Adoni-zedek king of Jerusalem sent unto Hoham king of Hebron, and unto Piram king of Jarmuth, and unto Japhia king of Lachish, and unto Debir king of Eglon, saying,

> Come up unto me, and help me, that we may smite Gibeon: for it hath made peace with Joshua and with the children of Israel [Josh. 10:1–4].

These kings hear of the treaty Gibeon made with Israel, and they come against these Hivites—for that is what these Gibeonites were—to destroy them.

> **Therefore the five kings of the Amorites, the king of Jerusalem, the king of Hebron, the king of Jarmuth, the king of Lachish, the king of Eglon, gathered themselves together, and went up, they and all their hosts, and encamped before Gibeon, and made war against it [Josh. 10:5].**

So what do these Gibeonites do?

> **And the men of Gibeon sent unto Joshua to the camp of Gilgal, saying, Slack not thy hand from thy servants; come up to us quickly, and save us, and help us: for all the kings of the Amorites that dwell in the mountains are gathered together against us [Josh. 10:6].**

They send an SOS to Joshua—come help us quickly!

> **So Joshua ascended from Gilgal, he, and all the people of war with him, and all the mighty men of valour.**

> **And the LORD said unto Joshua, Fear them not: for I have delivered them into thine hand; there shall not a man of them stand before thee.**

> **Joshua therefore came unto them suddenly, and went up from Gilgal all night [Josh. 10:7–9].**

Joshua came to their rescue for, I think, two reasons. First, because of the treaty, he felt obligated. Second, after all, he had been told to exterminate the enemy in that land. So his army took out after them. He used the tactic of surprise attack, and the Lord routed them before Israel.

> **Then spake Joshua to the LORD in the day when the LORD delivered up the Amorites before the children of Israel,**

and he said in the sight of Israel, Sun, stand thou still
upon Gibeon; and thou, Moon, in the valley of Ajalon.

And the sun stood still, and the moon stayed, until the
people had avenged themselves upon their enemies. Is
not this written in the book of Jasher? So the sun stood
still in the midst of heaven, and hasted not to go down
about a whole day.

And there was no day like that before it or after it, that
the Lord hearkened unto the voice of a man: for the Lord
fought for Israel [Josh. 10:12–14].

We have already discussed the various interpretations of Joshua's long
day in the opening remarks of this chapter. According to Joshua 10:12,
I believe God stopped the entire solar system to accomplish this miracle. The sun became silent. Joshua wanted more daylight in which to
fight; so God stopped the solar system and cut down the heat of the
sun by a hailstorm.

God caused the sun to stand still so that Joshua might be victorious
in battle. A certain professor once said, "It is ridiculous that God
would stop the entire universe for one man." It may sound preposter-
ous to some people, but God did it. He also sent His Son into the world
to die for sinners, which was much more wonderful than stopping the
sun. When God stopped the sun, He demonstrated His wisdom and
power. When He sent His Son into the world to become a man and die
on the cross, He displayed His love. If you were the only person that
had ever been born, Christ would have died for you. The professor will
say that is ridiculous also, and it is. But we have another word for it:
grace. "For by grace are ye saved through faith; and that not of yourselves: it is the gift of God" (Eph. 2:8).

VICTORY AT MAKKEDAH

And Joshua returned, and all Israel with him, unto the
camp to Gilgal.

But these five kings fled, and hid themselves in a cave at Makkedah.

And it was told Joshua, saying, The five kings are found hid in a cave at Makkedah.

And Joshua said, Roll great stones upon the mouth of the cave, and set men by it for to keep them:

And stay ye not, but pursue after your enemies, and smite the hindmost of them; suffer them not to enter into their cities: for the LORD your God hath delivered them into your hand [Josh. 10:15–19].

Remember that these kings and their people were given 420 years to make up their minds as to whether or not they would turn to God. Also God had made it known that He was giving the land to Israel and that He would save anyone who would turn to Him. Israel had to stay out of the land 420 years until the iniquity of the Amorites was full. That time had now come. God brought the children of Israel across the Red Sea not only for their sake, but also to demonstrate His redemption through power, as He had by blood that last night in Egypt when the angel of death passed over the homes on which the blood was on the doorposts. This was not only to convince the Egyptians that there was the living and true God amidst all the idols of Egypt, but also to convince these people in the land. Remember that the harlot Rahab had said, "For we have heard how the LORD dried up the water of the Red sea for you" (Josh. 2:10). She believed. Now if that woman believed, anybody could have believed God. However, these folks who are losing their lives did not believe. They had rejected God's mercy, and judgment is coming upon them. Friend, the message has never changed. God loves the world. God loves you and gave His Son. If you will believe on Him, you will not perish. Will you perish if you don't believe? Yes. That is what is happening to these folk. They just don't believe God. Now that may not sound nice to you, and you'd like to have it otherwise, but this is the way it is written in the Word of God.

> And it came to pass, when they brought out those kings
> unto Joshua, that Joshua called for all the men of Israel,
> and said unto the captains of the men of war which went
> with him, Come near, put your feet upon the necks of
> these kings. And they came near, and put their feet
> upon the necks of them.
>
> And Joshua said unto them, Fear not, nor be dismayed,
> be strong and of good courage: for thus shall the LORD
> do to all your enemies against whom ye fight [Josh.
> 10:24–25].

This is an impressive array of kings. Forty years prior to this time they caused Israelite spies to say, "We cannot enter the land. We will never be able to take it." Joshua had the captains of his army put their feet upon the necks of these kings to strengthen the heart of these people. They were frightened folk.

There was a whimsical story that came out of World War I when a certain hero, who had captured more German prisoners than any other, was being feted by some society folk in Nashville, Tennessee. One dear talkative dowager asked the hero, "How did you feel when you brought all of those soldiers in?" He replied, "I was scared to death!" This is how the Israelites felt. God wants to encourage them. Then Joshua slew the kings and hanged them on five trees.

> And it came to pass at the time of the going down of the
> sun, that Joshua commanded, and they took them down
> off the trees, and cast them into the cave wherein they
> had been hid, and laid great stones in the cave's mouth,
> which remain until this very day [Josh. 10:27].

The Israelites could have left the kings in the cave and starved them to death. It was more humane to slay them, and they did. They could not turn them loose, and they had no prison in which to put them. Do you think we live in a more civilized day? What do you think about the lawlessness on every hand in our country? We are not in a position to criticize what the Israelites did. They did not have lawlessness, and they settled their problem in the only way they could with a sinful, wicked race. If these kings had been turned loose, they would have led a rebellion against Joshua that would have caused literally thousands of people to die.

After the kings were hanged, they were taken down from the trees. They were not left hanging overnight. Why? Because we are told, "His body shall not remain all night upon the tree, but thou shalt in any wise bury him that day; (for he that is hanged is accursed of God;) that thy land be not defiled, which the LORD thy God giveth thee for an inheritance" (Deut. 21:23). In the New Testament Galatians 3:13 says, "Christ hath redeemed us from the curse of the law, being made a curse for us: for it is written, Cursed is every one that hangeth on a tree." Christ was crucified, but they took Him down from the cross because it is written that cursed is everyone that hangs on a tree. He bore the curse of sin for you and me.

> **And Joshua smote them from Kadesh-barnea even unto Gaza, and all the country of Goshen, even unto Gibeon.**
>
> **And all these kings and their land did Joshua take at one time, because the LORD God of Israel fought for Israel.**
>
> **And Joshua returned, and all Israel with him, unto the camp to Gilgal [Josh. 10:41–43].**

It is important to see that it is God who gave Israel victory and possession. Today our victory is in Christ. The victorious life is His life lived in us. Then we are blessed with all spiritual blessings, which are the possessions He has promised to us.

CHAPTERS 11 AND 12

THEME: The northern campaign and the roster of conquered kings

Chapter 11 contains the campaign in the north and the conclusion of Joshua's leadership in war.

> And it came to pass, when Jabin king of Hazor had heard those things, that he sent to Jobab king of Madon, and to the king of Shimron, and to the king of Achshaph,
>
> And to the kings that were on the north of the mountains, and of the plains south of Chinneroth, and in the valley, and in the borders of Dor on the west,
>
> And to the Canaanite on the east and on the west, and to the Amorite, and the Hittite, and the Perizzite, and the Jebusite in the mountains, and to the Hivite under Hermon in the land of Mizpeh.
>
> And they went out, they and all their hosts with them, much people, even as the sand that is upon the sea shore in multitude, with horses and chariots very many.
>
> And when all these kings were met together, they came and pitched together at the waters of Merom, to fight against Israel.
>
> And the Lord said unto Joshua, Be not afraid because of them: for tomorrow about this time will I deliver them up all slain before Israel: thou shalt hough their horses, and burn their chariots with fire [Josh. 11:1–6].

Jabin of Hazor in the north seems to have been the organizer. He sends out word to all the folk in that area to come against Joshua, because it is obvious now that he has overcome in the south and he is going to move to the north. And if he moves to the north, he will invade their land—which, of course, is exactly what he did.

As we have seen, Joshua's strategy was to split the land in two, then move into the south (which couldn't get help, you see, from the north). Now the northern kings come together.

> **So Joshua came, and all the people of war with him, against them by the waters of Merom suddenly; and they fell upon them [Josh. 11:7].**

Joshua's strategy, after dividing the land in two, was to come upon the enemy suddenly. You will see that Alexander the Great and also Napoleon used these same tactics.

> **Joshua made war a long time with all those kings.**

> **There was not a city that made peace with the children of Israel, save the Hivites the inhabitants of Gibeon: all other they took in battle [Josh. 11:18–19].**

It was a long and bitter campaign.

Now in chapter 12 we are given the names of the kings which Israel conquered. Frankly, a chapter like this is not very exciting to me. But the thing that impresses me is the detail that the God of this universe has given in items like this. We would think that He would constantly be dealing with great issues in grandiose terms, but God gets right down to the nitty-gritty where you and I live.

There is a lesson for us here. You and I sometimes hesitate to take to God in prayer the little details of our lives. We think, *I ought not to talk to Him about things like that.* Well, friend, talk to Him about those things. He wants to hear them.

A professor who was very liberal in his theology, said to me one time, "You take the Bible literally." "Yes," I said. "You certainly don't believe that God has books up there that He is going to open and look at." I think I shocked him when I said, "I sure do." He keeps the record, friend. Here is a chapter about these kings. I know nothing about them, but God does. He has the record.

He has two books: the Book of Works and the Lamb's Book of Life. Your name is written in one of them, my friend. It is written in the Book of Life when you trust Jesus Christ as your Savior. Your name will never be written there by your own effort. If your name is in this book, you have eternal life in Christ.

There is also a Book of Works. It records the details of everything you have ever done. It is going to be embarrassing for many people when they discover that all they did was give a cup of cold water that cost them nothing.

Recently a dear brother, a retired preacher with plenty of time on his hands, wrote me a twelve-page letter. I read it and much of the contents were meaningless to me. It mentioned places, people, and a church I knew nothing about. But God knows everything about that man and his life. He has it all written down. It is interesting to God. It adds real dimension to this life to realize that each little detail about His children is important to Him.

CHAPTER 13

THEME: Confirmation of land to the two and one-half tribes

Now Joshua was old and stricken in years; and the LORD said unto him, Thou art old and stricken in years, and there remaineth yet very much land to be possessed [Josh. 13:1].

We have passed only the halfway point in this book and we find that Joshua is already an old man and stricken in years. He is not going to be able to lead the children of Israel much longer. He is the leader God used to take the land, but the wars are over. He was about eighty years old when God called him, and now he is over one hundred years old. He had led Israel for many years. Time seems to have passed more quickly since Israel is in the land. The wilderness journey, by comparison, seemed long and drawn out. Now that Israel is in the land of milk and honey, they are laying hold of their possessions, and time passes quickly.

Friend, time would not pass so slowly for some people if they were living a life for God. My, how fast the time goes when you are serving Him! When I began my last pastorate, I was still a young man, and the twenty-one years just slipped by. Suddenly I discovered I was an old man and ready to retire. The most thrilling part of my ministry, however, has taken place since I retired. In my radio and conference ministry I have seen more results than at any time in my ministry. I have seen more of the hand of God, and I have been more conscious of His leading than at any time of my life. I think Joshua felt the same way.

From all outward appearances Israel seemed to be doing very well. They went into the land and drove a wedge right into the center of it. They conquered the south and went on to conquer the north, but the Lord reminded Joshua that there remained much land to be possessed. After doing a tremendous job, my friend, that will be true of you and me. It has been true of every servant of God; he will never accomplish all that he wished. In Philippians 3:12 Paul says, "Not as though I had already attained, either were already perfect: but I follow after, if that I may apprehend that for which also I am apprehended of Christ Jesus." God told Joshua that the land upon which the children of Israel walked would be theirs. They did not, however, walk on all of it. Neither will we ever be able to possess all of our spiritual possessions. I have met a few saints who think they have. They think there is nothing more for them to learn or do. They are satisfied with the life they are leading and have no desire to press on to ". . . the prize of the high calling of God in Christ Jesus" (Phil. 3:14).

The command of Joshua is terminated. He is no longer General Joshua. His next duty is to divide the land and especially to make sure that Moses' promises to the two and one-half tribes are confirmed.

> **Now therefore divide this land for an inheritance unto the nine tribes, and the half tribe of Manasseh,**
>
> **With whom the Reubenites and the Gadites have received their inheritance, which Moses gave them, beyond Jordan eastward, even as Moses the servant of the Lord gave them [Josh. 13:7–8].**

Joshua's commission (Josh. 1:6) not only included the subjugation of the land, but also the apportioning of it. He allocated not only those portions of Canaan that had already been conquered, but also those parts that were yet to be taken.

CHAPTER 14

THEME: Caleb given Hebron

The nine tribes and the half tribe are to have their inheritance by lot. Caleb, by privilege, obtains Hebron. Caleb, who was born a slave, was a spy with Joshua and brought back a favorable report the first time Israel came to Kadesh-barnea. According to Joshua 14:11 Caleb had found the fountain of youth. He had: (1) Faith to forget the past; (2) Faith to face facts; and (3) Faith to face the future.

> **And these are the countries which the children of Israel inherited in the land of Canaan, which Eleazar the priest, and Joshua the son of Nun, and the heads of the fathers of the tribes of the children of Israel, distributed for inheritance to them.**

> **By lot was their inheritance, as the LORD commanded by the hand of Moses, for the nine tribes, and for the half tribe [Josh. 14:1–2].**

As you will see by the map, all the way from Dan to Beersheba the land is divided into tribes. Reuben, Gad, and the half tribe of Manasseh are on the east bank of the Jordan River. Then starting in the south and going north we have the tribes of Simeon, Judah, Benjamin, Dan, Ephraim, Manasseh, Issachar, Zebulun, Naphtali, Asher, and Dan.

> **As the LORD commanded Moses, so the children of Israel did, and they divided the land.**

> **Then the children of Judah came unto Joshua in Gilgal: and Caleb the son of Jephunneh the Kenezite said unto him, Thou knowest the thing that the LORD said unto Moses the man of God concerning me and thee in Kadesh-barnea.**

> Forty years old was I when Moses the servant of the LORD
> sent me from Kadesh-barnea to espy out the land; and I
> brought him word again as it was in mine heart.
>
> Nevertheless my brethren that went up with me made
> the heart of the people melt: but I wholly followed the
> LORD my God [Josh. 14:5–8].

Caleb was a man who "wholly followed the LORD." If you want a recipe
for a long life and a good life, here it is.

> And now, behold, the LORD hath kept me alive, as he
> said, these forty and five years, even since the LORD
> spake this word unto Moses, while the children of Israel
> wandered in the wilderness: and now, lo, I am this day
> fourscore and five years old.
>
> As yet I am as strong this day as I was in the day that
> Moses sent me: as my strength was then, even so is my
> strength now, for war, both to go out, and to come in
> [Josh. 14:10–11].

Caleb is now eighty-five years old, and yet he can say that he is as
strong as the day Moses sent him into Canaan as a spy! During the
wilderness journey all of the first generation that came out of Egypt
died except Caleb and Joshua. These men, along with ten other spies,
brought back reports concerning the land of Canaan. The question
was, "Could Israel conquer the land?" Joshua and Caleb were certain
that with God's help Israel would be victorious in taking the land. The
other ten spies saw giants in the land and wanted to return to Egypt.
They wanted to go back to slavery, brickyards, the lash of the taskmas-
ters, chains, shackles, and groaning under burdens. The Lord Jesus
said, ". . . No man, having put his hand to the plough, and looking
back, is fit for the kingdom of God" (Luke 9:62). God had called Israel
to go into the land of Canaan, and Caleb believed it could be done.

During those forty years I suppose that often someone would say to

Caleb, "Oh, brother Caleb, isn't it terrible out here in this wilderness! It is so hot—it's 118° today!" Caleb would say, "I really hadn't noticed. I guess it is pretty warm, but I was thinking about those grapes of Eschol that I saw. And I was thinking about the city of Hebron. Our father Abraham liked that place, and I like it. That's where I am going." Caleb, even in the wilderness, could think of the future. He had a great hope. It kept him young. Those forty years in the wilderness killed off the rest of the crowd, but they didn't do a thing to him but make him healthy. They grew old, and he grew young. The giants in the Promised Land made the others tremble—they thought of themselves as grasshoppers. But Caleb thought of God. There was freedom from fear in the heart of this man. As Martin Luther said, "One with God is a majority." God was bigger than the giants.

Caleb reminds me of Adoniram Judson, the missionary who spent twelve years in Burma without a convert. The board that sent him out didn't sense the situation nor what a tremendous missionary they had in Judson; so they wrote him a very diplomatic letter, suggesting that he should come home. They asked him what the prospects in Burma were for the future. His reply was, "The future is as bright as the promises of God." His confidence in God was the reason he could stay in the wilderness of Burma all those years. Although he suffered a great deal and it took a long time for revival to break out, it finally did. His time was well spent.

Are you enjoying all the spiritual blessings that God has for you today? You say, "I have lots of trouble." I know that Christians have many troubles in the course of their lives. My heart goes out to them. But I always think of the testimony of a Negro man who said his favorite Bible verse was, "It came to pass." When puzzled people asked him what he meant by that, he replied, "When I get into trouble and problems pile up, I turn to my verse and know my troubles have not come to stay; they have come to pass." There are a lot of things you can complain about, friend, and I do my share also, but what about your hope? What about the future? Caleb for forty years in that wilderness was enjoying all the spiritual blessings that were his.

Because Caleb believed God and was a man of faith, he said:

> Now therefore give me this mountain, whereof the LORD
> spake in that day; for thou heardest in that day how the
> Anakims were there, and that the cities were great and
> fenced: if so be the LORD will be with me, then I shall be
> able to drive them out, as the LORD said [Josh. 14:12].

You will recall in Genesis that Abraham went to Hebron which means
"communion." It was a place of fellowship. Caleb had fellowship with
God and now he wants to reside at Hebron.

> And Joshua blessed him, and gave unto Caleb the son of
> Jephunneh Hebron for an inheritance.

> Hebron therefore became the inheritance of Caleb the
> son of Jephunneh the Kenezite unto this day, because
> that he wholly followed the LORD God of Israel [Josh.
> 14:13–14].

Friend, someday we will be rewarded. We will not be rewarded according to the great amount of work done for God, nor according to our
prominence and popularity. The important thing will be—did you
wholly follow the Lord? Oh, that God's people would learn today that
the most important thing in this life is to wholly follow the Lord! Caleb, man of God that he was, took Hebron. There were giants there, but
he said, "That's the place I want. That's the very best spot!" Oh, that
you and I might press toward the mark for the high calling of God in
Christ Jesus.

CHAPTERS 15—19

THEME: Consignment of land to the tribes of Israel

This section includes the apportionment of the Promised Land given to the tribes that settled on the west side of the Jordan River. Chapter 15 deals with Judah's portion; chapter 16 with Ephraim's portion; chapter 17 with Manasseh's portion; and chapters 18 and 19 with the portions of Simeon, Zebulun, Issachar, Asher, Naphtali, and Dan.

As important as this section was to the nation of Israel, it has no great significance to us. Therefore we shall lift out only the high points.

PORTION OF JUDAH

In chapter 14 we saw that Caleb was a member of the tribe of Judah and that God gave to him the city of Hebron. In chapter 15 we have more about this remarkable man. Also the boundaries of the entire tribe of Judah are given in this chapter.

> **And unto Caleb the son of Jephunneh he gave a part among the children of Judah, according to the commandment of the LORD to Joshua, even the city of Arba the father of Anak, which city is Hebron.**
>
> **And Caleb drove thence the three sons of Anak, Sheshai, and Ahiman, and Talmai, the children of Anak [Josh. 15:13–14].**

You see, the land old Caleb wanted was in giant country, and he was as ready to take on the giants now as when he was a young man.

> **And he went up thence to the inhabitants of Debir: and the name of Debir before was Kirjath-sepher.**

> And Caleb said, he that smiteth Kirjath-sepher, and tak-eth it, to him will I give Achsah my daughter to wife.
>
> And Othniel the son of Kenaz, the brother of Caleb, took it: and he gave him Achsah his daughter to wife.
>
> And it came to pass, as she came unto him, that she moved him to ask of her father a field: and she lighted off her ass; and Caleb said unto her, What wouldest thou?
>
> Who answered, Give me a blessing; for thou hast given me a south land; give me also springs of water. And he gave her the upper springs, and the nether springs [Josh. 15:15–19].

The total area of the tribe of Judah is marked out in the first of the chapter; then cities are mentioned. You'll have difficulty finding most of them on your map because they are way down in Negev.

PORTION OF EPHRAIM

Joseph was one of the twelve sons of Jacob, and his two sons, Ephraim and Manasseh, were each counted as a tribe. Because the tribe of Levi was the priestly tribe and was given no land, the total number of tribes inheriting the land was still only twelve tribes, rather than thirteen.

> And the lot of the children of Joseph fell from Jordan by Jericho, unto the water of Jericho on the east, to the wilderness that goeth up from Jericho throughout mount Beth-el,
>
> And goeth out from Beth-el to Luz, and passeth along unto the borders of Archi to Ataroth,
>
> And goeth down westward to the coast of Japhleti, unto the coast of Beth-horon the nether, and to Gezer: and the goings out thereof are at the sea.

So the children of Joseph, Manasseh and Ephraim, took their inheritance [Josh. 16:1–4].

PORTION OF MANASSEH

As you may recall, the tribe of Manasseh was divided. Half of the tribe settled on the east bank of the Jordan, but the other half crossed over and are now given their portion.

There is a remarkable instance in this chapter concerning the children of Joseph, and Ephraim in particular.

And the children of Joseph spake unto Joshua, saying, Why hast thou given me but one lot and one portion to inherit, seeing I am a great people, forasmuch as the LORD hath blessed me hitherto? [Josh. 17:14].

Ephraim was complaining because they had not been given a very large portion of land. In fact, Ephraim was given only about half of what Manasseh received. There were many people in the tribe of Ephraim. Joshua belonged to this tribe, and the Ephraimites probably felt that he would do something to help. Joshua, however, did nothing. The land they inherited was mountainous. The country is as rugged as any through which I have traveled. They were not satisfied.

And Joshua answered them, If thou be a great people, then get thee up to the wood country, and cut down for thyself there in the land of the Perizzites and of the giants, if mount Ephraim be too narrow for thee [Josh. 17:15].

If you travel to this area today, you will find that the hills are as bare as they are in Southern California. What happened to all of the trees? The enemies that have come into this country down through the centuries have completely denuded the hills. There is a great campaign in Israel right now to plant trees in that region. When I visited there, I planted five trees; one for myself, one for my wife, one for my daughter, one for the church in which I served, and one for a Jewish friend. Trees will grow here because the land was once covered with them.

By the way, in Christ's day the Mount of Olives was also covered with trees. If there had been just a little clump of trees, as there is today, His enemies would not have had any trouble finding Christ and His followers in the garden. Judas was needed to lead them through the jungle of trees and point out exactly where our Lord was.

Joshua's reply to his own tribe was noble.

> **And Joshua spake unto the house of Joseph, even to Ephraim and to Manasseh, saying, Thou art a great people, and hast great power: thou shalt not have one lot only:**
>
> **But the mountain shall be thine; for it is a wood, and thou shalt cut it down: and the outgoings of it shall be thine: for thou shalt drive out the Canaanites, though they have iron chariots, and though they be strong [Josh. 17:17–18].**

Joshua says, "If you don't like what you have, go up and possess the mountains. But remember there are giants in the land. You'll have to work; you'll have to fight. It's going to cost you something."

It is time we stopped complaining and possessed more land.

A great preacher from New York City once took a vacation in northern New York state. He went to church on Sunday in a small country town, and to his surprise the young pastor was preaching almost verbatim one of his published sermons. When the young man came out of the pulpit, and was greeting people at the door, the visiting pastor shook hands with him and asked, "Young man, I enjoyed your sermon this morning. How long did it take you to prepare it?" "Oh, it took me only about three hours," came his reply. "That is strange," said the famous preacher. "It took me about eight hours to prepare it."

It takes work to lay hold of spiritual possessions and blessings. Many years ago a student of mine entered the active ministry. He served in a church about three years and then came to see me. He was in distress because he said he was all preached out. I asked him how

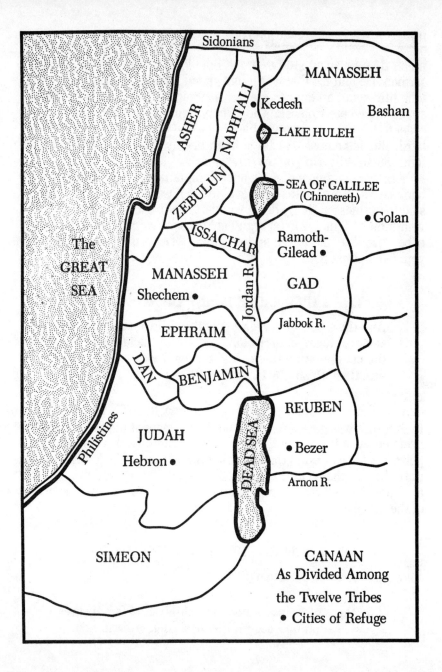

Sidonians

MANASSEH

ASHER

NAPHTALI

• Kedesh

Bashan

LAKE HULEH

ZEBULUN

SEA OF GALILEE
(Chinnereth)

ISSACHAR

• Golan

The
GREAT
SEA

MANASSEH

Shechem •

Ramoth-
Gilead •

Jordan R.

GAD

EPHRAIM

Jabbok R.

DAN

BENJAMIN

REUBEN

Philistines

JUDAH

Hebron •

DEAD SEA

• Bezer

Arnon R.

SIMEON

CANAAN
As Divided Among
the Twelve Tribes
• Cities of Refuge

much time he spent studying and how long it took him to prepare a
sermon. He told me that he did not spend much time studying, and it
took him about an hour to prepare a sermon. That was his problem. I
spend anywhere from eight to twenty hours preparing a sermon. In
order to lay hold of spiritual blessings, you are going to have to work
hard. But remember that there is an enemy. There are giants in the
land. Satan will trip you up if he can.

Another classmate of mine once complained to a professor about a
book he was required to read. He claimed it was as dry as dust. "Well,"
said the professor, "why don't you dampen it with a little sweat from
your brow?" This is a great argument for hard work. Joshua says to his
tribe, "Don't come to me and complain. There is plenty of land for
you. Go and get it."

THE TABERNACLE IS SET UP AT SHILOH

**And the whole congregation of the children of Israel as-
sembled together at Shiloh, and set up the tabernacle of
the congregation there. And the land was subdued before them [Josh. 18:1].**

The children of Israel pitched the tabernacle at Shiloh, a town in
Ephraim. It was not, however, to be the permanent place for the tabernacle because it was not the center of the land. God would choose a
permanent site through David, which would one day be Jerusalem. But
until the site changed, the children of Israel were to worship the Lord
at Shiloh. The tabernacle remained in Shiloh during the whole period
of the Judges.

DIVISION OF THE REMAINING LAND

Now Joshua gives a challenge.

**And there remained among the children of Israel seven
tribes, which had not yet received their inheritance.**

> And Joshua said unto the children of Israel, How long
> are ye slack to go to possess the land, which the LORD
> God of your fathers hath given you? [Josh. 18:2–3].

Seven of the tribes were standing around with their hands in their
pockets. They said to Joshua, "What about this land? What are you
going to give us?" Joshua told them, "You have been given a certain
area. Go and possess your land. How long are you going to wait?"

This is also God's challenge to us. He has made available to us all
spiritual blessings, but we are slack when it comes to claiming them.
God has been so good to us. Oh, how we can thank Him for His grace,
His love, His goodness, and His mercy. How wonderful He is! Why
don't we move in and possess the land He has given to us?

After Joshua's challenge, the tribes began to move out and possess
the land which had been allotted to them.

PORTION FOR BENJAMIN

The tribe of Benjamin received its inheritance between the land of
Judah and the tribes of Ephraim and Dan.

PORTION FOR SIMEON

> Out of the portion of the children of Judah was the inher-
> itance of the children of Simeon: for the part of the chil-
> dren of Judah was too much for them: therefore the
> children of Simeon had their inheritance within the in-
> heritance of them [Josh. 19:9].

As we saw in chapter 15, the tribe of Judah was given a special prefer-
ence because it was the kingly tribe. It will be in that tribe that the
capital of the nation, both religious and political, will be established.
The capital city will become Jerusalem, and we will see that David is
the one who made that choice.

Because the land allotted to Judah was more than it needed, the
southern portion was given to Simeon.

PORTION FOR ZEBULUN, ISSACHAR,
ASHER, NAPHTALI, DAN

The tribe of Zebulun received a portion of land that was landlocked in lower Galilee. The inheritance of Issachar went from Mount Tabor on the west to the southern part of the Sea of Galilee. It also included territory in the coastal region from north of Mount Carmel to the approximate area of Tyre and Sidon. The tribe of Naphtali settled in the area of eastern Upper and Lower Galilee. The territory of Dan was located between Benjamin and the Mediterranean Sea. Later some of the Danites migrated northward and settled near the northern part of Naphtali.

This section reveals how much detail God gave concerning Israel and the land. The land and the people go together. God not only gave them the land of Canaan, He also gave a particular area to a particular tribe. He gave each tribe a certain section of land. God was concerned about each individual and his possession.

In this God has a lesson for you and me today. It tells us that God is concerned about our personal lives. My friend, for Him your private life is not private—He knows you like a book. A rather godless neighbor said to me one day, "I want to go out into the desert where I can be by myself, and away from everybody." Well, that is a normal desire. We all need to get away from people once in awhile. But I reminded him—and I don't think he appreciated it—that he wouldn't get away from God. I said, "You can't run away from Him, brother. He will be right out there in the desert waiting for you." It is wonderful, friend, to get away from people like that, if we are getting away for fellowship with the Lord.

JOSHUA RECEIVES A SPECIAL PORTION

When they had made an end of dividing the land for inheritance by their coasts, the children of Israel gave an inheritance to Joshua the son of Nun among them:

According to the word of the LORD they gave him the city which he asked, even Timnath-serah in mount Ephraim: and he built the city, and dwelt therein.

These are the inheritances, which Eleazar the priest, and Joshua the son of Nun, and the heads of the fathers of the tribes of the children of Israel, divided for an inheritance by lot in Shiloh before the LORD, at the door of the tabernacle of the congregation. So they made an end of dividing the country [Josh. 19:49–51].

You would think that because Joshua was a man of God, had successfully led the children of Israel against the Canaanites, and had been victorious, that the Israelites would tell him that he could pick out any spot he wanted in which to settle. But that is not what happened. The Israelites did not offer him the choice spots in which to settle. Joshua made his own choice. It was a place called Timnath-serah. It was about eleven miles from Shiloh. It was a barren place, and one of the worst spots Joshua could have chosen. It reminds me of Abraham and Lot when they returned from the land of Egypt. Abraham said to Lot, "You pick any section you want and I will take what is left of this land." Lot took the very best and left Abraham holding the bag. This incident shows the character of these men. Joshua chose land that was similar to the backside of the desert. This is certainly a revelation of his character. It also reveals something about the Israelites. They were perfectly willing to let this man of God have a small, barren place as his portion.

In my opinion it is equally as shameful to see a church or Christian organization that has been served by a faithful worker, let that worker grow old and retire without making any arrangement for a pension for him. Cold-blooded business corporations take care of their employees when they retire, but God's people often fail to do this.

CHAPTER 20

The cities of refuge set before us a vivid scene which has a remarkable lesson for us. God gave to the children of Israel a commandment regarding setting aside certain cities for refuge. It is interesting that many tribes and many primitive people have had this same thing. Evidently this is something that was passed on to all mankind. The cities of refuge were for the protection of one who had killed another accidentally.

In the Hawaiian Islands, on the Kona coast of the Big Island, there is a place known as the City of Refuge. It was in use back in the days before Christianity came to the Islands, when the tribes were slaying each other and even offering human sacrifices. It is there as a tourist attraction today.

God's commandment for the establishment of cities of refuge was first given in Exodus 21:13: "And if a man lie not in wait, but God deliver him into his hand; then I will appoint thee a place whither he shall flee." Then explicit directions for the cities of refuge are given in Numbers 35—the entire chapter. "Then ye shall appoint you cities to be cities of refuge for you; that the slayer may flee thither, which killeth any person at unawares" (Num. 35:11).

Now that the children of Israel are in the Promised Land and each tribe has been allotted its portion of land, the Lord speaks to Joshua about assigning certain cities to be cities of refuge.

> **Speak to the children of Israel, saying, Appoint out for you cities of refuge, whereof I spake unto you by the hand of Moses:**
>
> **That the slayer that killeth any person unawares and unwittingly may flee thither: and they shall be your refuge from the avenger of blood [Josh. 20:2–3].**

If one man killed another, it would be one of two things. It would either be manslaughter—that is, the killing of another accidentally, or it would be premeditated murder. In Israel a murderer would be stoned to death. If in our society we had capital punishment for murder, with no "ifs" and "ands" about it, and the man who was guilty was executed quickly, it would save countless lives. We wouldn't be seeing our police officers shot down or storekeepers held up and murdered without mercy. My friend, God knows human nature. This was His law. However, if one killed another unintentionally, without premeditation, he is to be provided protection. There is an example given in Scripture of two men out in the woods, cutting down a tree. The axe head comes off the handle and strikes one of the men and kills him. Suppose the brother of the slain man says, "I know that man had it in for my brother. He did that purposely. I'm going to kill him!" That man wouldn't have a chance unless there was a place of refuge. So the man who had been responsible for the death would be given the opportunity of running to one of the cities of refuge.

> **And when he that doth flee unto one of those cities shall stand at the entering of the gate of the city, and shall declare his cause in the ears of the elders of that city, they shall take him into the city unto them, and give him a place, that he may dwell among them.**
>
> **And if the avenger of blood pursue after him, then they shall not deliver the slayer up into his hand; because he smote his neighbour unwittingly, and hated him not beforetime.**
>
> **And he shall dwell in that city, until he stand before the congregation for judgment, and until the death of the high priest that shall be in those days: then shall the slayer return, and come unto his own city, and unto his own house, unto the city from whence he fled [Josh. 20:4–6].**

The city of refuge has a great spiritual lesson for you and me. The Lord Jesus Christ was slain. And the Scripture makes it clear that not only was the Lord Jesus Christ slain, but He is our city of refuge today. Speaking of Christ as our refuge, the writer of Hebrews says, "who have fled for refuge to lay hold upon the hope set before us." The reference, of course, is to those who, though conscious of their own sinfulness, have availed themselves of the salvation that was secured for them by our Lord upon the cross. All who find a refuge in Him are saved forever from the judgment of a holy God.

Now who is guilty of slaying Christ? The whole world is guilty. Both Jew and Gentile stand guilty before God as having participated in that which brought about the death of His Son. But Christ came to give Himself a ransom for all. And His sacrifice on the cross has opened up, as it were, a city of refuge for all who put their trust in Him.

It is absolutely wrong to try to blame the Jew for the crucifixion of Christ. He was not crucified on a Jewish cross; He was crucified on a Roman cross. But it is useless to pin the blame on any one people. One racial group is as guilty as another. We all are in the same position. We are all guilty.

Peter, in his second sermon to his Jewish brethren, said, "And now, brethren, I wot that through ignorance ye did it, as did also your rulers. But those things, which God before had shewed by the mouth of all his prophets, that Christ should suffer, he hath so fulfilled" (Acts 3:17–18). Therefore Peter could say to them, "Repent ye therefore, and be converted."

The apostle Paul makes it clear that the Gentiles are also guilty. "Howbeit we speak wisdom among them that are perfect: yet not the wisdom of this world, nor of the princes of this world, that come to nought. . . . Which none of the princes of this world knew: for had they known it, they would not have crucified the Lord of glory" (1 Cor. 2:6, 8).

According to these passages, God looks upon the whole world as guilty of the sin of manslaughter in connection with the death of Christ. To be specific, you are guilty. But you can point the finger right back at me and say, "You are guilty." But, thank God, His death made a city of refuge, a place for you and me to come.

As the song writer, George Keith, put it,

> How firm a foundation, ye saints of the Lord
> Is laid for your faith in His excellent Word!

What more can He say than to you He hath said,
To you who for refuge to Jesus have fled?

Have you fled to Jesus for refuge? There is protection there. What a wonderful chapter this is!

CHAPTER 21

THEME: Cities for Levites

The Levites were not given any land as were the other tribes. Instead they were scattered out so that they could minister to the people. Levi was the priestly tribe.

> Then came near the heads of the fathers of the Levites unto Eleazar the priest, and unto Joshua the son of Nun, and unto the heads of the fathers of the tribes of the children of Israel;
>
> And they spake unto them at Shiloh in the land of Canaan, saying, The LORD commanded by the hand of Moses to give us cities to dwell in, with the suburbs thereof for our cattle [Josh. 21:1–2].

Apparently they had a suburban problem in that day also. The Levites were to be given forty cities in which to dwell—all the way from Dan in the north to Beer-sheba in the south.

The division of the land is completed now.

> And the LORD gave unto Israel all the land which he sware to give unto their fathers; and they possessed it, and dwelt therein.
>
> And the LORD gave them rest round about, according to all that he sware unto their fathers: and there stood not a man of all their enemies before them; the LORD delivered all their enemies into their hand [Josh. 21:43–44].

The children of Israel now possessed the land of Canaan, but that was only a small segment of the land God had promised them. If they are to get any more land, they will have to go and possess it. The rule still stands that every place their feet stand upon will be theirs. That which the Israelites possess now, however, is free from the enemy and they can enter into rest.

The rest for us today is the rest of redemption. It is the rest that we desperately need. We live in an age of tension. There are many pressures, and if there is one thing that the average Christian needs, it is to enter into the rest God has provided.

As we shall see as we move into the Book of Judges, Israel failed to completely rid her possession of her enemies. Why? Because of her unbelief. Even Joshua could not give them the rest they needed since they failed to believe God and appropriate His power.

The writer of the Hebrews warns us about repeating Israel's failure: "There remaineth therefore a rest to the people of God. For he that is entered into his rest, he also hath ceased from his own works, as God did from his. Let us labour therefore to enter into that rest, lest any man fall after the same example of unbelief" (Heb. 4:9–11). How do you and I enter into that rest? By faith, that is the only way.

At the time of Christ, when Israel rejected Him as King and He rejected their cities, He gave a personal invitation which stands yet today, "Come unto me, all ye that labour and are heavy laden, and I will give you rest" (Matt. 11:28). That rest is the rest of redemption.

Now here in Joshua 21 the people have entered into the rest—at least temporarily—which God had provided for them. My, how wonderful it must have been after the long, weary journey through the wilderness and the warfare to take their possessions, to settle down on their own parcel of ground. What a thrill it must have been to cultivate it and eat the fruits of it.

CHAPTER 22

THEME: The two and one-half tribes are sent home; they build the altar of witness

As you will recall, the two and one-half tribes did not take their inheritance in the land with the other tribes. They remained on the east side of the Jordan River. They could have the inheritance they wanted only if they sent their armies into the land to help conquer it. This is what they did and, when the battle was won, they were free to return home.

Then Joshua called the Reubenites, and the Gadites, and the half tribe of Manasseh,

And said unto them, Ye have kept all that Moses the servant of the LORD commanded you, and have obeyed my voice in all that I commanded you:

Ye have not left your brethren these many days unto this day, but have kept the charge of the commandment of the LORD your God [Josh. 22:1–3].

Just before the two and one-half tribes leave, Joshua calls them together and commends them for a job well done. He tells them that they have done a fine thing by helping their brethren. Then he gives them a warning.

But take diligent heed to do the commandment and the law, which Moses the servant of the LORD charged you, to love the LORD your God, and to walk in all his ways, and to keep his commandments, and to cleave unto him, and to serve him with all your heart and with all your soul [Josh. 22:5].

These tribes are warned that even though they have chosen to dwell on the wrong side of the Jordan, they are still to follow the Mosaic system. After Joshua warns them about their duty, he dismisses them with a blessing.

> **So Joshua blessed them, and sent them away: and they went unto their tents [Josh. 22:6].**

The two and one-half tribes returned home.

> **And when they came unto the borders of Jordan, that are in the land of Canaan, the children of Reuben and the children of Gad and the half tribe of Manasseh built there an altar by Jordan, a great altar to see to [Josh. 22:10].**

They apparently built this altar on the west side of the Jordan River. It was an altar "to see to." This is a strange expression. Literally it means an altar "great to sight." This means that it could be seen from a great distance. It was an imposing structure. Bible scholars searched for the ruins of this altar on the east side of Jordan. But finally an archaeologist discovered the ruins on the west side of Jordan, and they are there today, located in a prominent place, a great altar in appearance. They built this monument to remind them of something. When the rest of the children of Israel heard what they had done, they became upset and gathered at Shiloh.

> **And when the children of Israel heard of it, the whole congregation of the children of Israel gathered themselves together at Shiloh, to go up to war against them [Josh. 22:12].**

The children of Israel believed the two and one-half tribes were building an altar upon which to offer sacrifices. They thought it was an attempt to divide the nation.

> Thus saith the whole congregation of the LORD, What
> trespass is this that ye have committed against the God
> of Israel, to turn away this day from following the LORD,
> in that ye have builded you an altar, that ye might rebel
> this day against the LORD?
>
> Is the iniquity of Peor too little for us, from which we are
> not cleansed until this day, although there was a plague
> in the congregation of the LORD [Josh. 22:16-17].

The children of Israel accused the two and one-half tribes of building an altar to Baal. They remembered the time that Balaam had caused Israel to sin by seducing them to marry Moabite women and commit spiritual adultery. At that time God had judged them severely, and they were afraid it was going to happen again.

However, the two and one-half tribes give a good explanation for what they had done.

> Then the children of Reuben and the children of Gad
> and the half tribe of Manasseh answered, and said unto
> the heads of the thousands of Israel,
>
> The LORD God of gods, the LORD God of gods, he know-
> eth, and Israel he shall know; if it be in rebellion, or if in
> transgression against the LORD, (save us not this day,)
>
> That we have built us an altar to turn from following the
> LORD, or if to offer thereon burnt offering or meat offer-
> ing, or if to offer peace offerings thereon, let the LORD
> himself require it [Josh. 22:21-23].

They had not built an altar for purpose of offering sacrifices. The altar was simply a reminder that they still belonged to the nation Israel. It may have been an enlarged model of the altar of burnt offering found in the tabernacle, but it was not intended for sacrifices.

And if we have not rather done it for fear of this thing, saying, In time to come your children might speak unto our children, saying, What have ye to do with the Lord God of Israel? [Josh. 22:24].

The two and one-half tribes were sincere in what they had done, and the nine and one-half tribes accepted their explanation.

And Phinehas the son of Eleazar the priest said unto the children of Reuben, and to the children of Gad, and to the children of Manasseh, This day we perceive that the Lord is among us, because ye have not committed this trespass against the Lord; now ye have delivered the children of Israel out of the hand of the Lord [Josh. 22:31].

The children of Israel realized that they had been hasty in accusing the two and one-half tribes. They remind me of some of us who are sometimes a little hasty. We say and do things we should not say and do, and we are sincere in thinking we are defending the Word of God when in reality we are not. The children of Israel made a mistake in coming against their brethren with thoughts of war.

And the children of Reuben and the children of Gad called the altar Ed: for it shall be a witness between us that the Lord is God [Josh. 22:34].

On the surface, the building of this altar sounds like a good idea, and many commentators have placed their seal of approval upon it. However, let's take more than a cursory look at this altar called "Ed." In the tabernacle was the brazen altar for sacrifices. There was to be no other. Deuteronomy 12:27 says, "And thou shalt offer thy burnt offerings, the flesh and the blood, upon the altar of the Lord thy God: and the blood of thy sacrifices shall be poured out upon the altar of the Lord thy God, and thou shalt eat the flesh." Israel was told to destroy all other altars. "But ye shall destroy their altars, break their images, and cut down their groves" (Exod. 34:13). There was to be but one exception, in Deuteronomy 27:4–8, where Israel is told to take twelve stones out of the Jordan River and put them up as a memorial. The two and one-half tribes never crossed over Jordan, and the river actually divided them from their brethren. This altar recognized that division. This altar was prima facie evidence that they were divided. It made way for the division later on. Right now Israel is divided east and west. It is nine and one-half tribes versus two and one-half tribes at this point, but later on it will be a north and south division with ten tribes in the north against two tribes in the south.

The brazen altar in the tabernacle, typifying the redemptive work of Christ, was a place of unity. And friend, I can meet with any man who will exalt Jesus Christ. In John 17:20–21 Jesus prayed, "Neither pray I for these alone, but for them also which shall believe on me through their word; That they all may be one; as thou, Father, art in me, and I in thee, that they also may be one in us: that the world may believe that thou hast sent me." There is an organic unity of those who are in Christ. The altar speaks of the death of Christ as a sacrifice.

As the two and one-half tribes built a bloodless altar which had divided Israel, today those who are liberal in their theology have divided the church. They have accused fundamentalists of being schismatic, but it is liberalism that has departed from the cross and the deity of Christ. They do not like an altar with blood. They have put up an "Ed," if you please. They worship at an altar where no sacrifice is to be offered. They have a "bloodless" Christ. Like the two and one-half tribes, their conduct reveals that they have departed from the truth. Our Lord said, "Ye shall know them by their fruits . . ." (Matt. 7:16). Several hundred years later the Lord Jesus crossed the Sea of Galilee and came to the country of the Gadarenes. The people living there were from the tribe of Gad, and they were still living on the wrong side of the Jordan River. Our Lord came upon a demon-possessed man dwelling in the tombs, and He cast the demons out of the man and gave them permission to enter a herd of pigs nearby. The Gadarenes were in the pig business! Can you imagine an Orthodox Jew in the pig business? They had failed to follow the commandments of God. They were on the wrong side of Jordan.

Liberalism has indeed divided the church. It has erected a beautiful altar, a "bloodless" Christ, one who never actually lived, one without deity, one without ability to save humanity.

My friend, have you crossed over Jordan? Have you entered into the rest of redemption which Christ offers?

CHAPTERS 23 AND 24

THEME: The last message of Joshua

In chapter 23 Joshua calls the leaders of Israel to courage and certainty. Then in chapter 24 he calls to the tribes of Israel for consecration and consideration of the covenant of God. The chapter closes with the death of Joshua.

A deathbed message is becoming very familiar in the Word of God. You recall that Jacob called his twelve sons about him and gave prophecies concerning each of them. Then Moses called the twelve tribes—the sons are now tribes—to him and blessed them. Now Joshua, who has been their leader for forty years there in the Land of Promise, is giving them his final message before his death.

> **And it came to pass a long time after that the LORD had given rest unto Israel from all their enemies round about, that Joshua waxed old and stricken in age.**
>
> **And Joshua called for all Israel, and for their elders, and for their heads, and for their judges, and for their officers, and said unto them, I am old and stricken in age:**
>
> **And ye have seen all that the LORD your God hath done unto all these nations because of you; for the LORD your God is he that hath fought for you [Josh. 23:1–3].**

You will notice that Joshua calls the people about him and says, "I am now ready to retire; I am a senior citizen, and I have some final words for you. You have seen what God has done for you."

> **Behold, I have divided unto you by lot these nations that remain, to be an inheritance for your tribes, from Jor-**

> dan, with all the nations that I have cut off, even unto the great sea westward.
>
> And the Lord your God, he shall expel them from before you, and drive them from out of your sight; and ye shall possess their land, as the Lord your God hath promised unto you.
>
> Be ye therefore very courageous to keep and to do all that is written in the book of the law of Moses, that ye turn not aside therefrom to the right hand or to the left [Josh. 23:4-6].

Joshua is calling them to do what Moses had called them to do.

> That ye come not among these nations, these that remain among you; neither make mention of the names of their gods, nor cause to swear by them, neither serve them, nor bow yourselves unto them:
>
> But cleave unto the Lord your God, as ye have done unto this day [Josh. 23:7-8].

The grave danger of crossing the Jordan River, facing an enemy in a strange land, encountering the unknown on every hand, and meeting fear on every side, had kept Israel close to the Lord. Joshua recognized that now, since they had entered into rest and were enjoying prosperity and plenty, they would drift away from God. That is the story of human nature. It never changes.

At the time of this writing, I feel that the United States is facing a similar situation. After World War II, I was disturbed that God had judged Europe and even Russia and Korea. How these nations suffered, but we came through unscathed! While other nations went through a period of hardship, our nation entered an era of prosperity and affluence. I could not understand why God did not judge us. Then I realized that He was testing us with prosperity. The most dangerous period any people can go through is not the time of grave danger and suffering, but the time of peace and plenty.

This is the reason Joshua is giving Israel this charge. "God has done these wonderful things for you; now stay close to Him, and obey Him. If you do this, God will continue to bless you." Then he warns them what will happen if they turn from their God.

> **Take good heed therefore unto yourselves, that ye love the LORD your God.**
>
> **Else if ye do in any wise go back, and cleave unto the remnant of these nations, even these that remain among you, and shall make marriages with them, and go in unto them, and they to you:**
>
> **Know for a certainty that the LORD your God will no more drive out any of these nations from before you; but they shall be snares and traps unto you, and scourges in your sides, and thorns in your eyes, until ye perish from off this good land which the LORD your God hath given you [Josh. 23:11–13].**

He warns that God's judgment would be upon them.

> **Therefore it shall come to pass, that as all good things are come upon you, which the LORD your God promised you; so shall the LORD bring upon you all evil things, until he have destroyed you from off this good land which the LORD your God hath given you.**
>
> **When ye have transgressed the covenant of the LORD your God, which he commanded you, and have gone and served other gods, and bowed yourselves to them; then shall the anger of the LORD be kindled against you, and ye shall perish quickly from off the good land which he hath given unto you [Josh. 23:15–16].**

This is more of a prediction than a warning. As we well know, this prediction is now history.

In chapter 24 Joshua again gathers the people together, and they present themselves before the Lord. Joshua relays to them God's review of their history and His gracious dealings with them.

> **And Joshua said unto all the people, Thus saith the LORD God of Israel, Your fathers dwelt on the other side of the flood in old time, even Terah, the father of Abraham, and the father of Nachor: and they served other gods [Josh. 24:2].**

This reveals something that we didn't know before, although we suspected it. When God called Abraham from Ur of the Chaldees, He called him out of a home of idolatry. Terah, his father, we are told here, served other gods.

This raises the question: Why did God choose Abraham and make a nation from him? Let's consider the background. After the Tower of Babel, man totally departed from the Lord. No one served God—not even Terah the father of Abraham. When God confused the language, the people scattered in every direction, and they took with them a knowledge of the true and living God, which is the reason even pagan tribes today have a knowledge of the true God, although they do not worship Him. There was total apostasy after Babel.

Now what will God do that will be consistent with His person, His attributes, and His character? He could judge the human family and remove it from the earth. He could make the earth as bleak as the moon if He wanted to. But He didn't. He will recover mankind. He will begin with one man. That man was Abraham, who must have had a desire in his heart to know the living and true God. When God called him, He told him to leave Ur and all his family. Now we know why. Terah was an idolater. God called him away from all that in order to deal with him and make of him a nation through which the Messiah would come into the world.

Now God formed the nation in the brickyards of Egypt. (And, friends, if God is going to make anything of you and me, He will take us through the fire to do it. He won't use the molly-coddle of our contemporary churches, I can assure you!)

I sent Moses also and Aaron, and I plagued Egypt, according to that which I did among them: and afterward I brought you out.

And I brought your fathers out of Egypt: and ye came unto the sea; and the Egyptians pursued after your fathers with chariots and horsemen unto the Red sea.

And when they cried unto the LORD, he put darkness between you and the Egyptians, and brought the sea upon them, and covered them; and your eyes have seen what I have done in Egypt: and ye dwelt in the wilderness a long season [Josh. 24:5–7].

God continues to trace His care of them: delivering them from the Amorites who fought them and from Balaam who tried to curse them, bringing them across the Jordan and delivering them from the inhabitants of the land who fought against them.

And I have given you a land for which ye did not labor, and cities which ye built not, and ye dwell in them; of the vineyards and oliveyards which ye planted not do ye eat [Josh. 24:13].

Now the people of Israel are settled in the land. But, because they did not get rid of the civilization that was there, they are surrounded by idolatry. They are in real danger. Realizing this, Joshua calls them to a real dedication to God, a turning over of their lives completely to Him. Listen to him.

Now therefore fear the LORD, and serve him in sincerity and in truth: and put away the gods which your fathers served on the other side of the flood, and in Egypt; and serve ye the LORD.

And if it seem evil unto you to serve the LORD, choose you this day whom ye will serve; whether the gods which your fathers served that were on the other side of

the flood, or the gods of the Amorites, in whose land ye
dwell: but as for me and my house, we will serve the
LORD [Josh. 24:14–15].

The more I know about Joshua, the better I like him. Through the years
he has stood in the shadow of Moses so that we think he is a sort of
miniature Moses. But Joshua is a man of great stature. God made no
mistake in choosing this man. Although Joshua is an average man,
this book reveals that an average man dedicated to God can be mightily used. He says to the nation, "Do you want to go back to the gods of
your fathers, those pagan gods which they served? Or do you want to
serve the gods of the Amorites? You can choose. But as for me and my
house, we have made our choice; we are going to serve the Lord!"
Friend, this was a tremendous challenge to all the tribes of Israel to
consider their covenant with God.
    Notice the response of the people.

And the people answered and said, God forbid that we
should forsake the LORD, to serve other gods;

For the LORD our God, he it is that brought us up and our
fathers out of the land of Egypt, from the house of bondage, and which did those great signs in our sight, and
preserved us in all the way wherein we went, and
among all the people through whom we passed [Josh.
24:16–17].

You would think that because of the fantastic way God worked with
Israel they would stay close to Him and serve Him. It is easy to point a
finger back about 3,580 years ago and say what a sorry lot Israel was.
What terrible failures they were. What about us today? How close are
we staying to the living God?

If ye forsake the LORD, and serve strange gods, then he
will turn and do you hurt, and consume you, after that
he hath done you good [Josh. 24:20].

God also has been so good to us that many people live in a lackadaisical manner without any regard as to the blessings He has showered upon them. Many people think they can do exactly as they please. It is true that He is a God of mercy, love, and comfort, but He is also a God of judgment.

> And the people said unto Joshua, Nay; but we will serve the LORD [Josh. 24:21].

These sound like good intentions on the part of Israel, don't they?

> So Joshua made a covenant with the people that day, and set them a statute and an ordinance in Shechem.
>
> And Joshua wrote these words in the book of the law of God, and took a great stone, and set it up there under an oak, that was by the sanctuary of the LORD [Josh. 24:25–26].

In other words, what Joshua wrote was put on the same scroll that contained the five books of Moses.

This brings us to the death of Joshua.

> And it came to pass after these things, that Joshua the son of Nun, the servant of the LORD, died, being an hundred and ten years old.
>
> And they buried him in the border of his inheritance in Timnath-serah, which is in mount Ephraim, on the north side of the hill of Gaash [Josh. 24:29–30].

Joshua was buried in that barren place he had chosen for his inheritance.

> And Israel served the LORD all the days of Joshua, and all the days of the elders that overlived Joshua, and

> which had known all the works of the LORD, that he had
> done for Israel.
>
> And the bones of Joseph, which the children of Israel
> brought up out of Egypt, buried they in Shechem, in a
> parcel of ground which Jacob bought of the sons of Ha-
> mor the father of Shechem for an hundred pieces of sil-
> ver: and it became the inheritance of the children of
> Joseph [Josh. 24:31–32].

At the time of Joshua's death he must have been held in high esteem because Israel served the Lord all the days of Joshua. This was the effect of his godly influence.

Joseph was the father of Ephraim and Manasseh. When these two sons left Egypt, they brought their father's bones with them and carried them for forty years in the wilderness. They had promised Joseph they would bury his bones in the Promised Land. Why? Because he was expecting to be raised from the dead in that land.

> And Eleazar the son of Aaron died; and they buried him
> in a hill that pertained to Phinehas his son, which was
> given him in mount Ephraim [Josh. 24:33].

Aaron was the first priest to die; Eleazar was the second. The Book of Joshua is bound by death. It begins with the death of Moses and ends with the deaths of Joshua and Eleazar.

The thing that interests me in this verse, however, is the fact that they buried Eleazar in the hill that pertained to Phinehas, his son, which was given him in Mount Ephraim. The question is, "Where did Phinehas get this land?" The priests were given no land, and yet this man acquired a nice little parcel of real estate. Here is a beginning of departure from the living and true God, which will become obvious in the Book of Judges.

(For Bibliography to Joshua, see Bibliography at the end of Judges.)

JUDGES

The Book of

JUDGES

INTRODUCTION

The Book of Judges takes its title from the twelve men and one woman who served as judges during the period from Joshua's death to the time of Samuel.

This book was written during the period of the monarchy, judging by the phrase which occurs four times, "In those days there was no king in Israel." It is possible that it was written by Samuel, but the actual writer is unknown.

All the judges were themselves limited in their capabilities. In fact, each one seemed to have some defect and handicap which was not a hindrance but became a positive asset under the sovereign direction of God. None of them were national leaders who appealed to the total nation as Moses and Joshua had done. The record is not continuous but rather a spotty account of a local judge in a limited section of the nation.

Backsliding and the amazing grace of God in recovering and restoring is the theme of Judges. *The New Scofield Reference Bible* gives the theme of the Book of Judges as "Defeat and Deliverance." This is unusually appropriate. There is, however, another aspect which this book emphasizes: disappointment.

The children of Israel entered the Land of Promise with high hopes and exuberant expectation. You would expect these people—who were delivered out of Egypt, led through the wilderness for forty years, and brought into the land with such demonstration of God's power and direction—to attain a high level of living and victory in the land, and in their lives. Such was not the case. They failed ignobly and suffered miserable defeat after defeat.

The Book of Judges is a philosophy of history. "Righteousness exalteth a nation: but sin is a reproach to any people" (Prov. 14:34).

1. Historically it records the history of the nation from the death of Joshua to Samuel, who was the last of the judges and the first of the prophets. It bridges the gap between Joshua and the rise of the monarchy. There was no leader to take Joshua's place in the way he had taken Moses' place. This was the trial period of the theocracy after they entered the land.

2. Morally it is the time of the deep declension of the people as they turned from God, the unseen Leader, and descended to the low level of "In those days there was no king in Israel: every man did that which was right in his own eyes" (compare Jud. 1:1 with 20:18). This should have been an era of glowing progress, but it was a dark day of repeated failure.

The "hoop" of Israel's history begins with the nation serving God. Then they take certain steps downward. They did evil in the sight of the Lord and served Baalim (see Jud. 2:11). They forsook the Lord, and

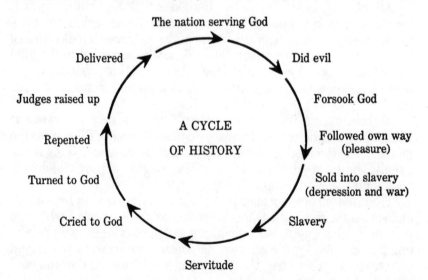

they served Baal and Ashtaroth. The anger of the Lord was hot against Israel, and He delivered them into the hands of their enemies. Israel entered a time of servitude. Soon Israel cried out to God in their sad plight and distress. They turned to God and repented. God heard their prayers and raised up judges through whom they were delivered. Then again the nation served God.

Soon the same old story repeated itself. The children of Israel did evil, forsook God, followed their own pleasure, were sold into slavery, entered a period of servitude, cried out to God in their distress, turned to Him, judges were raised up, and Israel was delivered. The nation began serving God again, and they were once again at the top of the cycle. My friend, the hoop of history just turns over and over. You can follow that hoop right through the Bible, and it is still turning today. The old bromide "history repeats itself" is absolutely true.

The Book of Isaiah opens with God giving this philosophy of history. Isaiah outlines three steps that cause the downfall of nations: (1) spiritual apostasy; (2) moral awfulness; and (3) political anarchy, which is the final stage of any nation. These steps have destroyed nations down through history.

If you want to know just how up-to-date the Book of Judges is, listen to the words of the late General Douglas MacArthur: "In this day of gathering storms, as moral deterioration of political power spreads its growing infection, it is essential that every spiritual force be mobilized to defend and preserve the religious base upon which this nation is founded; for it has been that base which has been the motivating impulse to our moral and national growth. History fails to record a single precedent in which nations subject to moral decay have not passed into political and economic decline. There has been either a spiritual reawakening to overcome the moral lapse, or a progressive deterioration leading to ultimate national disaster."

OUTLINE

I. **Introduction to the Era of the Judges, Chapters 1—2**
  A. Condition of Nation after Death of Joshua (Revealed in Limited Victories of Tribes of Judah, Simeon, Benjamin, Manasseh, Ephraim, Zebulun, Asher, Naphtali, Dan), Chapter 1
  B. God Feeds into Computer of History Israel's Cycle in Period of the Judges, Chapter 2

II. **Era of the Judges, Chapters 3—16**
  A. 1st Apostasy; Conquered by Mesopotamia; Delivered through Othniel, the Judge, 3:1–11
  B. 2nd Apostasy; Conquered by Moabites and Philistines; Delivered through Ehud and Shamgar, the Judges, 3:12–31
  C. 3rd Apostasy; Conquered by Jabin, King of Canaan, Delivered through Deborah and Barak, the Judges, 4:1—5:31
  D. 4th Apostasy; Conquered by Midian; Delivered through Gideon, the Judge 6:1—8:32
  E. 5th Apostasy; Civil War; Delivered through Abimelech, Tola, Jair, the Judges, 8:33—10:5
  F. 6th Apostasy; Conquered by Philistines and Ammonites; Delivered through Jephthah, Ibzan, Elon, Abdon, the Judges, 10:6—12:15
  G. 7th Apostasy; Conquered by Philistines; Delivered Partially through Samson, the Judge, Chapters 13—16

III. **Results of the Era of the Judges (Confusion), Chapters 17—21**
  A. Religious Apostasy (The Temple), Chapters 17—18
  B. Moral Awfulness (The Home), Chapter 19
  C. Political Anarchy (The State), Chapters 20—21

CHAPTERS 1 AND 2

THEME: Introduction to the era of the judges

Mentioned are nine of the twelve tribes, in chapter 1, in their failure to win a total victory in driving out the enemy. The three tribes not mentioned are Reuben, Issachar, and Gad. It must be assumed that they likewise failed. Each tribe faced a particular enemy. At no time was the entire nation engaged in a warfare against any particular enemy. The weakness of the tribes is first revealed in verse 3 where Judah called upon Simeon for help in his local situation.

THE CONDITION OF ISRAEL AFTER THE DEATH OF JOSHUA

Now after the death of Joshua it came to pass, that the children of Israel asked the Lord, saying, Who shall go up for us against the Canaanites first, to fight against them? [Jud. 1:1].

The weakness of the tribes is revealed from the word *go*. They asked the Lord what they should do and who would go for them against the Canaanites. The Canaanites were well entrenched in the land because the Israelites had failed to drive them out. They were a thorn in Israel's side during the reigns of Saul and David.

And the Lord said, Judah shall go up: behold, I have delivered the land into his hand [Jud. 1:2].

The Canaanites, apparently, were the principal enemy.

And Judah said unto Simeon his brother, Come up with me into my lot, that we may fight against the Canaanites; and I likewise will go with thee into thy lot. So Simeon went with him [Jud. 1:3].

At first this looks like a fine sign of cooperation between Judah and Simeon, and it was, but it was also a sign of weakness. The tribe of Judah had no business asking for help to drive the Canaanites out of their particular portion of land. With God's help they should have been able to do it. As a result, the Canaanites were never completely driven out of the land.

> And Judah went up; and the LORD delivered the Canaan-ites and the Perizzites into their hand: and they slew of them in Bezek ten thousand men [Jud. 1:4].

You would think that after this first step of victory the people in Judah would be confident that God would deliver their inheritance into their hands.

> And afterward the children of Judah went down to fight against the Canaanites, that dwelt in the mountain, and in the south, and in the valley.
>
> And Judah went against the Canaanites that dwelt in Hebron: (now the name of Hebron before was Kirjath-arba:) and they slew Sheshai, and Ahiman, and Talmai.
>
> And from thence he went against the inhabitants of De-bir: and the name of Debir before was Kirjath-sepher [Jud. 1:9–11].

The town *Debir* was a center of culture for the Canaanite people. It is called the "town of books." I guess the library was there.

> And Caleb said, He that smiteth Kirjath-sepher, and tak-eth it, to him will I give Achsah my daughter to wife.
>
> And Othniel the son of Kenaz, Caleb's younger brother, took it: and he gave him Achsah his daughter to wife [Jud. 1:12–13].

Israel first took the hill country and held it the longest. The foothills, lying between the hill country and the coast, were the scene of con-stant fighting between Israel and the Canaanites. When the children of

Israel settled in the Promised Land, they were subject to the influence and temptations of the Canaanite religion. It was a degrading religion, and they soon lapsed into idolatry and apostasy.

Whoever took this city was promised a reward, and in this case it was Caleb's daughter, Achsah. Grammatically, Othniel can be either Caleb's nephew or younger brother, but his marriage to Achsah would also classify him as a son-in-law. He undoubtedly was chosen as a judge because of his relationship to Caleb. Nepotism was prevalent even in that day. If he had been the son-in-law of Joe Doakes, he probably would never have become a judge. Many men today occupy positions of prominence, not because of their ability, but because of a certain relationship or circumstance. Napoleon called himself a man of destiny. He became prominent because of the times in which he was born. If he had lived in our generation, probably he would have been unknown. So it was with Othniel.

Nine of the twelve tribes mentioned in this chapter are mentioned in connection with failure. We have looked at the tribes of Judah and Simeon, and now Benjamin and Manasseh are the next to be considered. Failure is something that persisted in each one of the tribes.

> **And the children of Benjamin did not drive out the Jebusites that inhabited Jerusalem; but the Jebusites dwell with the children of Benjamin in Jerusalem unto this day [Jud. 1:21].**

That is, at the time this record was written.

> **Neither did Manasseh drive out the inhabitants of Beth-shean and her towns, nor Taanach and her towns, nor the inhabitants of Dor and her towns, nor the inhabitants of Ibleam and her towns, nor the inhabitants of Megiddo and her towns: but the Canaanites would dwell in that land.**

> **And it came to pass, when Israel was strong, that they put the Canaanites to tribute, and did not utterly drive them out.**

> Neither did Ephraim drive out the Canaanites that dwelt in Gezer; but the Canaanites dwelt in Gezer among them.
>
> Neither did Zebulun drive out the inhabitants of Kitron, nor the inhabitants of Nahalol; but the Canaanites dwelt among them, and became tributaries [Jud. 1:27–30].

The report is failure for each of them.

> Neither did Asher drive out the inhabitants of Accho, nor the inhabitants of Zidon, nor of Ahlab, nor of Achzib, nor of Helbah, nor of Aphik, nor of Rehob:
>
> But the Asherites dwelt among the Canaanites, the inhabitants of the land: for they did not drive them out.
>
> Neither did Naphtali drive out the inhabitants of Bethshemesh, nor the inhabitants of Beth-anath; but he dwelt among the Canaanites, the inhabitants of the land: nevertheless the inhabitants of Beth-shemesh and of Beth-anath became tributaries unto them [Jud. 1:31–33].

And they chased Dan up into the hill country.

> And the Amorites forced the children of Dan into the mountain: for they would not suffer them to come down to the valley [Jud. 1:34].

This is the Promised Land—God had given it to them! Yet not one tribe, apparently, was able to possess the land that God had given to it. How tragic!

THE CHILDREN OF ISRAEL ARE REBUKED
FOR THEIR DISOBEDIENCE

> And an angel of the LORD came up from Gilgal to Bochim, and said, I made you to go up out of Egypt, and

have brought you unto the land which I sware unto your
fathers; and I said, I will never break my covenant with
you.

And ye shall make no league with the inhabitants of this
land; ye shall throw down their altars: but ye have not
obeyed my voice: why have ye done this?

Wherefore I also said, I will not drive them out from
before you; but they shall be as thorns in your sides, and
their gods shall be a snare unto you [Jud. 2:1–3].

I believe that the "angel of the Lord" is none other than the pre-
incarnate Christ. God appeared in a form that could be perceived by
the human senses. Although He had always met the need of His people, they had not obeyed His voice. This is the beginning of Israel's
"hoop of history." They repeated the weary round of forsaking God,
sinning, being reduced to servitude by the enemy, returning to God in
repentance, being delivered by God-appointed judges, back to obedience to God.

GOD RAISES UP JUDGES

Nevertheless the LORD raised up judges, which delivered
them out of the hand of those that spoiled them [Jud.
2:16].

Each time the nation hit bottom, God raised up a judge to deliver
them.

CHAPTER 3

THEME: First and second apostasy; God delivers Israel from servitude through her judges: Othniel, Ehud, and Shamgar

The children of Israel intermarried with the Canaanites, Hittites, Amorites, Perizzites, Hivites, and Jebusites among whom they lived. Israel did evil, forgot God, and served Baalim. God delivered them into slavery.

Othniel, the first judge, was raised up to deliver them. His only qualification seems to be that he was the nephew of Caleb and married his daughter.

Ehud, the second judge, was raised up to deliver Israel from the servitude of Eglon, king of Moab. His qualification was his being left-handed, which enabled him to gain the presence of the king without his concealed dagger being discovered.

Shamgar was the third judge, who was an expert with an ox goad. He used it as an instrument of war against the Philistines to deliver Israel.

All of the judges had some defect, some odd characteristic, or handicap which God used. The judges reveal that God can use any man who is willing to be used.

THE IDOLATRY OF ISRAEL BRINGS SERVITUDE

Now these are the nations which the LORD left, to prove Israel by them, even as many of Israel as had not known all the wars of Canaan;

Only that the generations of the children of Israel might know, to teach them war, at the least such as before knew nothing thereof;

Namely, five lords of the Philistines, and all the Canaanites, and the Sidonians, and the Hivites that dwelt in

> mount Lebanon, from mount Baal-hermon unto the en-
> tering in of Hamath [Jud. 3:1–3].

We find here that the Israelites had intermarried with the Canaanites, the Hittites, the Amorites, the Perizzites, the Hivites, and the Jebusites. They married into all the tribes, even though God had strictly forbidden it.

The five lords of the Philistines and the other tribes mentioned in this passage were enemies of the Israelites. As we proceed through the Old Testament, these enemies will appear time and time again. They were indeed a thorn in the flesh of the nation Israel.

> And the children of Israel dwelt among the Canaanites, Hittites, and Amorites, and Perizzites, and Hivites, and Jebusites:
>
> And they took their daughters to be their wives, and gave their daughters to their sons, and served their gods.
>
> And the children of Israel did evil in the sight of the Lord, and forgat the Lord their God, and served Baalim and the groves [Jud. 3:5–7].

Instead of driving the Canaanites from the land, Israel shared it with them. Instead of maintaining their own beliefs and worship of God, they intermarried with the Canaanites and adopted their religious beliefs. The children of Israel lapsed into a period of apostasy.

> Therefore the anger of the Lord was hot against Israel, and he sold them into the hand of Chushan-rishathaim king of Mesopotamia: and the children of Israel served Chushan-rishathaim eight years [Jud. 3:8].

Israel's idolatry resulted in chastisement. God sold them into slavery for eight years. They were oppressed to the point that they cried out to the Lord for help.

OTHNIEL, THE FIRST JUDGE

And when the children of Israel cried unto the LORD, the LORD raised up a deliverer to the children of Israel, who delivered them, even Othniel the son of Kenaz, Caleb's younger brother [Jud. 3:9].

How gracious and compassionate the Lord is! When the children of Israel cried unto Him for deliverance, He raised up Othniel to be the first judge.

And the spirit of the LORD came upon him, and he judged Israel, and went out to war: and the LORD delivered Chushan-rishathaim king of Mesopotamia into his hand; and his hand prevailed against Chushan-rishathaim.

And the land had rest forty years. And Othniel the son of Kenaz died [Jud. 3:10–11].

Othniel was the first and one of the better judges. There is no great criticism leveled against him. He saved his people from the oppression of Chushan-rishathaim. The only thing is that he was not capable in himself. He did not become leader of Israel because of his outstanding ability but because he was Caleb's nephew and had married Caleb's daughter. And yet God used him. It is amazing what kind of men God will use. Maybe that is the reason He can use you and me. This book should certainly encourage us, friend.

All of the judges were "little men." There was not a big one in the lot. These men were used of God because they were—and I have to say it—odd characters. Their very oddness caused God to use them.

The biography of Othniel was that he was the son of Kenaz, who was Caleb's brother. The Spirit of God came upon him, and he delivered the children of Israel from oppression. He died. In a very few verses we have the life and death of this man. He had a lot going for him, but there was no glamour or anything spectacular connected with his life. Most biographies are much like this.

I met a man on the streets of Los Angeles, California years ago who had written several fine biographies of Christian leaders of the past. He was working on a book about a present-day Christian leader, and I asked him how the work was coming along. He told me that he was having difficulty keeping the front page from rubbing against the back page. Apart from the birth and death of the man, there was little to say about him. Engraved on the tombstone of a dentist were the words: "Dr. John Smith filling his last cavity." That not only applies to dentists but to the rest of us as well.

Othniel was an ordinary man, but God came upon his simple life and made it something worthwhile. God can also touch our ordinary lives and make them worthwhile.

EHUD, THE SECOND JUDGE

And the children of Israel did evil again in the sight of the Lord: and the Lord strengthened Eglon the king of Moab against Israel, because they had done evil in the sight of the Lord [Jud. 3:12].

Here goes the hoop rolling down through history again. The Israelites were serving God for awhile, then they turned their backs on Him and did evil in His sight.

Ehud was one of the judges God raised up to deliver Israel. He had very little ability. I cannot find that he did anything other than kill Eglon. He just happened to be left-handed, which gave him a marvelous opportunity to get rid of a man who was bringing all kinds of tragedy into the lives of the Israelites. Ehud was the instrument God used. His act of killing Eglon accomplished the purpose. God many times uses this method to cut out a cancer of sin in order to save the body of the people. Thousands of lives were saved because of what Ehud did.

Many people will say, "Well, our civilization would not permit something like this." No one can say this honestly, however, because we dropped an atomic bomb which killed men, women, and children. War is a terrible thing.

The remarkable fact is that the only advantage Ehud had was that he was left-handed. Friend, we don't have to have unusual ability to be used of God. Do you remember William Carey? He was a humble cobbler. Dwight L. Moody had little formal education. A friend gave me a cassette tape of Dwight L. Moody's voice, taken from a record. I had never realized what a wonderful voice he had—I would not have associated such a voice with the pictures I have seen of him. Although he did not have much of an education, he certainly sounded as though he did. Also I am reminded of G. Campbell Morgan. When he preached his first sermon in a particular church, he was turned down by the pulpit committee. They told him they did not think he could ever become a preacher. I certainly would have hated to have been responsible for that judgment because Dr. Morgan became one of the truly great Bible expositors of his time. All three of these men—Carey, Moody, Morgan—unpromising though they seemed, were mightily used by God.

Also there have been many men, humble men, who have been used by God in other capacities. J. C. Penney was the son of a preacher. When his father died, his mother was left without support because the church in that day did not provide a pension for a pastor's widow. He and his mother had to take in washing to exist. He resolved that some day he would make money to take care of his mother and also take care of poor preachers and their widows. Well, there is a place down in Florida named for Penney at which only retired preachers and their widows can live. God has used him in that way.

There is another man, a rancher, with whom I used to hunt down on the Brazos River. He told me that as a young fellow he had staked a claim way out in west Texas on land that was so bad nobody wanted it. The weather was so rough he had to move his family into town, and he would sleep at night on his saddle blanket with a slicker over him and a trench around him to let the water drain off. He said, "People think I was lucky to hit oil on that land, but I prayed that if God would enable me to keep it and make money, I'd use it for Him." He did just that. He established a fund that has supported many a missionary in South America.

> And he gathered unto him the children of Ammon and
> Amalek, and went and smote Israel, and possessed the
> city of palm trees [Jud. 3:13].

When the Israelites went against God's will, He delivered them into
servitude. Then what happened?

> So the children of Israel served Eglon the king of Moab
> eighteen years.

> But when the children of Israel cried unto the LORD, the
> LORD raised them up a deliverer, Ehud the son of Gera, a
> Benjamite, a man lefthanded: and by him the children
> of Israel sent a present unto Eglon the king of Moab
> [Jud. 3:14–15].

Here we go again. The hoop is rolling. Israel cried unto the Lord and
He raised up a deliverer. Who was he? He was Ehud, the son of Gera, a
Benjamite, a left-handed man. This is a good one for you, friends. The
only thing that this man had going for him was that he was left-
handed, a southpaw!

> But Ehud made him a dagger which had two edges, of a
> cubit length; and he did gird it under his raiment upon
> his right thigh.

> And he brought the present unto Eglon king of Moab:
> and Eglon was a very fat man.

> And when he had made an end to offer the present, he
> sent away the people that bare the present.

> But he himself turned again from the quarries that were
> by Gilgal, and said, I have a secret errand unto thee, O
> king: who said, Keep silence. And all that stood by him
> went out from him.

> And Ehud came unto him; and he was sitting in a sum-
> mer parlour, which he had for himself alone. And Ehud

said, I have a message from God unto thee. And he arose out of his seat.

And Ehud put forth his left hand, and took the dagger from his right thigh, and thrust it into his belly:

And the haft also went in after the blade; and the fat closed upon the blade, so that he could not draw the dagger out of his belly; and the dirt came out.

Then Ehud went forth through the porch, and shut the doors of the parlour upon him, and locked them [Jud. 3:16–23].

This is a brutal thing that took place. It certainly lacks the heroic or romantic. His name means "red hair" and he was left-handed. He made a dagger which had two edges, and he hid it under his clothes on his right side. Now don't miss that. He was left-handed and would have to reach over on his right side to pull out the dagger. In that day almost everybody was right-handed, and they were searched on the left side to see if they carried a weapon. The king's Secret Service agents searched Ehud on the wrong side. He gained entrance by bringing a "present," which was probably the tribute. Eglon was a big fat king. After Ehud had given him the present, he pretended he had a secret to tell him. The king sent everyone else out of the room, thinking he was going to hear a very secret message. Instead, a bloody thing was about to happen. At a convenient moment, Ehud took out the dagger and plunged it into the king. He stuck him like you would a pig. The dagger was covered by the king's fat. Then Ehud locked the doors and left.

Ehud's act was not a cowardly one. It took courage to do what he did.

When he was gone out, his servants came; and when they saw that, behold, the doors of the parlour were locked, they said, Surely he covereth his feet in his summer chamber.

**And they tarried till they were ashamed: and, behold,
he opened not the doors of the parlour; therefore they
took a key, and opened them: and, behold, their lord
was fallen down dead on the earth [Jud. 3:24–25].**

The servants of Eglon, king of Moab, waited around outside of the
king's door. They saw that the parlor doors were locked and thought
the king was asleep. They did not wish to disturb him. They kept
thinking he would wake up. They waited so long they were very em-
barrassed. What happened? They finally opened the doors with a key
and found Eglon dead.

**And Ehud escaped while they tarried, and passed be-
yond the quarries, and escaped unto Seirath [Jud. 3:26].**

All of the time the servants were waiting for their king to awaken, Ehud
had an opportunity to escape. He left the land of Moab and went to
another place, Seirath by name, where they could not find him.

**And it came to pass, when he was come, that he blew a
trumpet in the mountain of Ephraim, and the children
of Israel went down with him from the mount, and he
before them.**

**And he said unto them, Follow after me: for the Lord
hath delivered your enemies the Moabites into your
hand. And they went down after him, and took the fords
of Jordan toward Moab, and suffered not a man to pass
over.**

**And they slew of Moab at that time about ten thousand
men, all lusty, and all men of valour; and there escaped
not a man.**

**So Moab was subdued that day under the hand of Israel.
And the land had rest fourscore years [Jud. 3:27–30].**

SHAMGAR, THE THIRD JUDGE

As in the days of the judges, God still uses ordinary men who want to be used to accomplish His great purposes. God can use you if you want to be used, friends.

Now here is the third judge, Shamgar.

And after him was Shamgar the son of Anath, which slew of the Philistines six hundred men with an ox goad: and he also delivered Israel [Jud. 3:31].

In this case, it is not the man, it is the method that is remarkable. He used an ox goad, which is a very crude instrument. The Israelites just didn't have iron weapons; so he used that which he had.

I hear people say today, "Oh, we must have the best and the latest methods." It is fine to have good methods, but what about the message? It is wonderful to have airplanes that transport missionaries, but when the missionary gets to his field, is he giving out the Word of God? That's what I want to know. Television is great, but notice how it is prostituted today. The important thing is not the method, but the message.

An ox goad can be dedicated to God if it is in the right hands. Remember that God used the rod of Moses. He used a stone from the slingshot of David. And all Dorcas had was a needle and thread. Also there was a boy who had only five loaves and a few fishes. All of these things were given to God. Whatever you have, friend, if you will put it in His hand, He will use it. Think of these three judges who are mentioned in this chapter. They are three little men—plus God.

CHAPTER 4

THEME: Third apostasy; God delivers Israel from oppression through Deborah and Barak

DEBORAH AND BARAK

And the children of Israel again did evil in the sight of the LORD, when Ehud was dead.

And the LORD sold them into the hand of Jabin king of Canaan, that reigned in Hazor; the captain of whose host was Sisera, which dwelt in Harosheth of the Gentiles.

And the children of Israel cried unto the LORD: for he had nine hundred chariots of iron; and twenty years he mightily oppressed the children of Israel [Jud. 4:1–3].

After the death of Ehud, Israel again turned to idolatry, and a new period of oppression began. The Lord sold Israel into the hand of Jabin, king of Canaan. Sisera, captain of the host, had nine hundred chariots of iron. These chariots caused dread among the Israelites who had no such armaments. For twenty years Jabin oppressed Israel.

And Deborah, a prophetess, the wife of Lapidoth, she judged Israel at that time.

And she dwelt under the palm tree of Deborah between Ramah and Beth-el in mount Ephraim: and the children of Israel came up to her for judgment [Jud. 4:4–5].

Here we have a mother in Israel, Deborah, who is described as being both a prophetess and a judge. We are also told that she was the wife of Lapidoth, but I like to turn that around and say that Lapidoth was the husband of Deborah. She was quite a woman. She was raised up by

God to judge Israel, and she called upon the general to get busy. He was not doing his job. He should go against the enemy that Israel might be delivered from slavery.

> **And she sent and called Barak the son of Abinoam out of Kedesh-naphtali, and said unto him, Hath not the LORD God of Israel commanded, saying, Go and draw toward mount Tabor, and take with thee ten thousand men of the children of Naphtali and of the children of Zebulun?**
>
> **And I will draw unto thee to the river Kishon, Sisera, the captain of Jabin's army, with his chariots and his multitude; and I will deliver him into thine hand.**
>
> **And Barak said unto her, If thou wilt go with me, then I will go: but if thou wilt not go with me, then I will not go [Jud. 4:6–8].**

If there ever was a general who was a sissy, it was Barak. He should have been out in the thick of the battle, but here he is hiding behind a woman's skirt. Barak will not go into battle unless Deborah goes along. If this prophetess went with him, he felt he would be successful in battle. No wonder God had to use a woman in that day!

> **And she said, I will surely go with thee: notwithstanding the journey that thou takest shall not be for thine honour; for the LORD shall sell Sisera into the hand of a woman. And Deborah arose, and went with Barak to Kedesh [Jud. 4:9].**

Deborah promised to go with Barak but told him that a woman would be the heroine of the battle.

THE DEATH AND DEFEAT OF SISERA

Deborah was a forthright woman who, as we shall see, wanted deliverance for her people. Barak called together his army, and they got ready to go against the enemy. God gave them the victory.

> But Barak pursued after the chariots, and after the host, unto Harosheth of the Gentiles: and all the host of Sisera fell upon the edge of the sword; and there was not a man left [Jud. 4:16].

They exterminated the army.

> Howbeit Sisera fled away on his feet to the tent of Jael the wife of Heber the Kenite: for there was peace between Jabin the king of Hazor and the house of Heber the Kenite [Jud. 4:17].

She was a Gentile.

> And Jael went out to meet Sisera, and said unto him, Turn in, my lord, turn in to me; fear not. And when he had turned in unto her into the tent, she covered him with a mantle.
>
> And he said unto her, Give me, I pray thee, a little water to drink; for I am thirsty. And she opened a bottle of milk, and gave him drink, and covered him.
>
> Again he said unto her, Stand in the door of the tent, and it shall be, when any man doth come and inquire of thee, and say, Is there any man here? that thou shalt say, No.
>
> Then Jael Heber's wife took a nail of the tent, and took an hammer in her hand, and went softly unto him, and smote the nail into his temples, and fastened it into the ground: for he was fast asleep and weary. So he died [Jud. 4:18–21].

Since the rest of his army was destroyed, Sisera's primary desire was to save his own life. Apparently the Canaanites had not bothered the Kenites, and Sisera believed he would be safe among these people. He went to the house of Heber, and his wife Jael offered the weary soldier hospitality. Her kindness led him to believe he could trust her. When he went to sleep, she took a tent pin and hammer and let him have it, friends. She got rid of him. This brought a great deliverance for Israel.

CHAPTER 5

THEME: *The song of Deborah and Barak*

In the fourth chapter of Judges we saw the incident concerning Deborah. You will recall that they were dark days. In fact, it was dark all
over the land. The incident concerning Deborah, Barak, and Jael took
place in the northern part of Israel. God gave Israel a great deliverance.
This song is one of praise to God and a rehearsal of the entire episode.

> **Then sang Deborah and Barak the son of Abinoam on
> that day, saying,**
>
> **Praise ye the Lord for the avenging of Israel, when the
> people willingly offered themselves.**
>
> **Hear, O ye kings; give ear, O ye princes; I, even I, will
> sing unto the Lord; I will sing praise to the Lord God of
> Israel.**
>
> **Lord, when thou wentest out of Seir, when thou mar-
> chedst out of the field of Edom, the earth trembled, and
> the heavens dropped, the clouds also dropped water.**
>
> **The mountains melted from before the Lord, even that
> Sinai from before the Lord God of Israel [Jud. 5:1–5].**

Their song is very poetic, to be sure.

Deborah confesses that she is a mother in Israel and was not look-
ing for a job at all. The fact that she took the lead is no reflection on her.
She was God's choice. History affords many such examples. There was
Molly Pitcher, the wife of a Revolutionary soldier, who, at the battle of
Monmouth, manned the cannon at which her husband had just fallen.
Other examples are Joan of Arc, the French heroine, and Zenobia,
queen of Palmyra.

Deborah was one of the outstanding judges. She far exceeded

Othniel in ability. It is an evidence of decline, however, when women come into the position of authority. It is a sign of weakness and of a flabby age. We have already seen that weak-kneed general, Barak. He was a sissy. He wanted to stay way back behind the fighting lines. In fact, he wanted to stay home and did not want to fight at all. Deborah had to agree to go with him before he was willing to go and battle the enemy.

Many years ago I heard Dr. Harry Ironside tell of a woman who was preaching in a park as he and one of his friends were walking by. His friend said, "It is a shame for a woman to get up and preach like that. I deplore it. She should not be doing that." Dr. Ironside replied, "I agree with you that it is a shame, not that a woman is preaching, but that there is not a man to take her place."

Regardless of what you might think (and I know I may sound very out of date, especially in this day of women's rights), America is paying an awful price for taking women into its defense system and into industry. I made this statement as far back as 1948, and I am no prophet, but I predicted a backwash of immorality if women left the home. Well, it certainly came to pass. First there was an epidemic of women shooting their husbands, deserting their children, becoming dope peddlers, and committing suicide. There are many things that are considered a menace in our country—inflation, crime, foreign aggression—but I feel that the greatest danger is that women are leaving their place in the home.

Deborah actually did not want to leave her home. However, Jabin was king of the Canaanites, and God had sold Israel into slavery to them. When the time of deliverance came, Barak, who commanded Israel's army, did not want to go into battle. God, however, promised victory. The victory was won, but it was an ignominious victory for Barak.

After the battle Deborah and Barak sang a song that was one of the first songs of the human race.

In the days of Shamgar the son of Anath, in the days of Jael, the highways were unoccupied, and the travellers walked through byways.

**The inhabitants of the villages ceased, they ceased in
Israel, until that I Deborah arose, that I arose a mother
in Israel [Jud. 5:6-7].**

The song mentions Shamgar. He was the judge, you remember, that
used an ox goad. He had judged during a time of lawlessness and
grave immorality. It was not safe to walk the highways; the highways
were unoccupied. Travelers walked through the byways because it was
not safe to take the main route. It is becoming increasingly unsafe to
travel today also. Women do not dare walk the streets at night alone.
Deborah knew all about this kind of danger because lawlessness
reigned in her day.

Then her song mentions the lack of leadership. Rulers had ceased
to rule. There was no great man who could lead. Deborah was a
mother. She had a mother's heart. Very candidly, she did not want to
take the lead, but there was no man to assume the leadership. How
tragic was this situation. She wanted something better for her children
than what she saw about her. Because of her desire, she became a
judge in Israel. She stepped out and took the lead in a day when her
nation had denied God.

**They chose new gods; then was war in the gates: was
there a shield or spear seen among forty thousand in
Israel? [Jud. 5:8].**

Israel denied God—as men do today—only instead of becoming athe-
ists, they became polytheists. They began to worship many gods.
Think of the multitudes today that are living without God! Deborah
did not want her children to grow up this way and that is why she
stepped out as she did.

Do you remember the hopes that this country had after World War
II? Everyone in the United States thought they were going to have peace
at last. Many people thought they would live in peace and sin, and it
would be nice. They forgot to read Psalm 85:10 which says, "Mercy
and truth are met together; righteousness and peace have kissed each
other." Friend, peace and righteousness do not even speak to each other

today—I do not even think they know each other! It is interesting that
God did not let us live comfortably in peace and sin. God did not let
Israel live that way either. It is also interesting to note that Israel lacked
a defense. They had nothing with which to meet the enemy. Deborah
sang, ". . . then was war in the gates: was there a shield or spear seen
among forty thousand in Israel?" Israel had no help at all.

> **My heart is toward the governors of Israel, that offered
> themselves willingly among the people. Bless ye the
> LORD [Jud. 5:9].**

The conditions were not all bad. There were some godly rulers. Deborah wanted them to know that she gave them her support. It was the
godless crowd that she rejected.

> **Speak, ye that ride on white asses, ye that sit in judg-
> ment, and walk by the way.**
>
> **They that are delivered from the noise of archers in the
> places of drawing water, there shall they rehearse the
> righteous acts of the LORD, even the righteous acts
> toward the inhabitants of his villages in Israel: then
> shall the people of the LORD go down to the gates [Jud.
> 5:10–11].**

The gates were the place of assembly. Wherever people were going to
meet, instead of talking about the common topics of the day, as they
had in the past, they would talk about the righteous acts of God.

> **Awake, awake, Deborah: awake, awake, utter a song:
> arise, Barak, and lead thy captivity captive, thou son of
> Abinoam.**
>
> **Then he made him that remaineth have dominion over
> the nobles among the people: the LORD made me have
> dominion over the mighty [Jud. 5:12–13].**

After Israel's victory over the enemy, Deborah once again tells Barak to take command. But he does not take charge, and she has to continue as the leader. She found she had dominion over the mighty.

> **Out of Ephraim was there a root of them against Amalek; after thee, Benjamin, among thy people; out of Machir came down governors, and out of Zebulun they that handle the pen of the writer [Jud. 5:14].**

The tribes now join in.

> **And the princes of Issachar were with Deborah; even Issachar, and also Barak: he was sent on foot into the valley. For the divisions of Reuben there were great thoughts of heart.**
>
> **Why abodest thou among the sheepfolds, to hear the bleatings of the flocks? For the divisions of Reuben there were great searchings of heart [Jud. 5:15–16].**

Some of the tribes didn't help. Reuben sent no reinforcements to the battle. They were not there to lend support when it was badly needed. They were neighbors and close by, but they did nothing. They felt like they should stay with their flocks and apparently did not trust someone else to watch their animals. They acted as if there was no war. They burned their draft cards and did not come. The tribe of Issachar, on the other hand, stood with Deborah and Barak.

> **Gilead abode beyond Jordan: and why did Dan remain in ships? Asher continued on the sea shore, and abode in his breaches [Jud. 5:17].**

Dan was busy in commerce. The folk in that tribe did not want to come to the battle. Asher continued on the seashore. You know, human nature never changes. As in Deborah's day, many folk today have let their country down, and they should not have done that.

> **Zebulun and Naphtali were a people that jeoparded their lives unto the death in the high places of the field [Jud. 5:18].**

These two tribes really fought.

> **The kings came and fought, then fought the kings of Canaan in Taanach by the waters of Megiddo; they took no gain of money [Jud. 5:19].**

Israel had some allies that were formerly enemies. They helped at the waters of Megiddo which is near what will be Armageddon one day.

> **They fought from heaven; the stars in their courses fought against Sisera [Jud. 5:20].**

I don't believe this is merely a poetic expression. My feeling is that it could truly be said that heaven, that God was against this enemy.

> **The river of Kishon swept them away, that ancient river, the river Kishon. O my soul, thou hast trodden down strength.**
>
> **Then were the horsehoofs broken by the means of the prancings, the prancings of their mighty ones.**
>
> **Curse ye Meroz, said the angel of the LORD, curse ye bitterly the inhabitants thereof; because they came not to the help of the LORD, to the help of the LORD against the mighty [Jud. 5:21–23].**

Frankly, I cannot identify Meroz. However, one thing I know for sure and that is that I would not want to be an inhabitant of the city of Meroz. They did not come to help the work of the Lord and so they were cursed. Today, also, there are multitudes of folks who are not coming to help the work of the Lord.

Blessed above women shall Jael the wife of Heber the Kenite be, blessed shall she be above women in the tent [Jud. 5:24].

The heroine of the day was Jael, not Barak, in spite of her dastardly deed. But this was a time of war and the aftermath of war. All around was the holocaust of battle, broken bodies, and the fruit of war. Men's souls were blackened and scarred. The foliage of civilization was removed like thin veneer. Snarled and gnarled, the trunk of barbarianism was revealed. What Jael did was an awful thing. Woman has been created finer than man. There is something fine that has gone out of life today, and I think it centers in womanhood.

Now a mother's heart is revealed. Deborah remembers that Sisera, although he was the enemy, had a mother. And even though she extols Jael for what she did, she thinks of Sisera's mother.

The mother of Sisera looked out at a window, and cried through the lattice, Why is his chariot so long in coming? why tarry the wheels of his chariots?

Her wise ladies answered her, yea, she returned answer to herself,

Have they not sped? have they not divided the prey; to every man a damsel or two; to Sisera a prey of divers colours, a prey of divers colours of needlework, of divers colours of needlework on both sides, meet for the necks of them that take the spoil? [Jud. 5:28–30].

The mother of Sisera knew in her heart what had happened. She knew he had been slain. She had thought all of the time that he would be coming home, but he did not come. Even in this case, the heart of Deborah went out to this woman because she was a mother.

So let all thine enemies perish, O LORD: but let them that love him be as the sun when he goeth forth in his might. And the land had rest forty years [Jud. 5:31].

There have been mothers in the past who have overcome handicaps in evil days—evil days like those in which Deborah lived. Read the story of Augustine. He had a marvelous mother by the name of Monica, who prayed for him. He was a debauched college professor, and he finally came to the feet of Jesus Christ. There was also Susanna Wesley who prayed for her two sons, John and Charles Wesley. Now I am not talking about worshiping womanhood or motherhood, friend, but I do want to say that we are getting far away from God's conception of it. What a picture we have in Deborah and her song!

CHAPTERS 6—8

THEME: Fourth apostasy; God delivers Israel through Gideon

Gideon is the next judge. He is called to his position in chapter 6. Chapter 7 tells how mightily God used him. He is one of the most interesting judges, although not the most outstanding. In reality none of the judges were great. They were little people, marked by mediocrity. Each one was insignificant, insufficient, and inadequate. Each one had some aberration in his life. Each one of them had a glaring fault, and sometimes that fault was the very reason God chose them and used them.

I would like to add some background to this incident with some very pertinent facts. The account of the judges was discounted by the critics for many years. They said because it was not in secular history, these events actually did not take place, and there was no situation in the past into which they could be fitted. But all of that has changed now because of the spade of the archaeologist and the scholarly work of men like Burney, Moulton, Breasted, and Garstang. These outstanding conservative scholars have given us the background for the Book of Judges.

Now we know that at this particular time in history Egypt was weak, very weak. It had been a world power, but it was weak because the pharaohs who were in office were weak men. Also there were internal problems and troubles. As a result, this nation was losing its grip upon its colonies. The nomadic tribes to the east of the Dead Sea and to the south of the Dead Sea began to push in. They pushed in because there was a drought in their land. They had experienced it there for several years. So these nomadic tribes of the desert began to encroach upon the territory of Israel. The Midianites and the Amalekites were among the Bedouins of the desert who came into the land.

The story of Gideon opens with that.

ISRAEL SINS AND IS OPPRESSED BY MIDIAN

And the children of Israel did evil in the sight of the LORD: and the LORD delivered them into the hand of Midian seven years.

And the hand of Midian prevailed against Israel: and because of the Midianites the children of Israel made them the dens which are in the mountains, and caves, and strong holds [Jud. 6:1–2].

The Midianites and the Amalekites moved as a disorganized tribe. They were raiders. They would raid the crops and supplies of others. They generally took their families with them. In fact, they took all that they had with them. They would pitch their tents as they moved along. In this incident, we are not given numbers concerning them because no one in the world would have been able to number them—they were so disorganized. But by sheer numbers, and they were many, they overwhelmed the inhabitants of the land. The children of Israel fled from their homes and lived in caves and dens. There is abundant evidence in the land of Israel today that they lived in caves, especially during the period of the judges.

It is the same old story once again. Israel sinned and the hoop started moving. God had blessed the children of Israel under the administration of Deborah. When they sinned, God delivered them to Midian, and they cried out for deliverance.

For they came up with their cattle and their tents, and they came as grasshoppers for multitude; for both they and their camels were without number: and they entered into the land to destroy it [Jud. 6:5].

The Midianites came up against the children of Israel. They were like a plague of grasshoppers as they came into the land. They came "without number," which means that they had not been counted. They were such a large company that certainly the enemy could not count them.

The Midianites saw that Israel had good crops, and they needed grain and foodstuff for themselves and for their animals.

The tribe of Manasseh, of which Gideon was a member, occupied the plain in which was located the Plain of Esdraelon (the place where Armageddon will be fought). Although they had occupied that territory, when these nomads came into that area, they took to the hills; they moved into the dens and into the caves up there. They had to. They saw their crops which they had left all taken by the enemy. This is the historical period into which the story of Gideon is cast.

> **And it came to pass, when the children of Israel cried unto the Lord because of the Midianites,**
>
> **That the Lord sent a prophet unto the children of Israel, which said unto them, Thus saith the Lord God of Israel, I brought you up from Egypt, and brought you forth out of the house of bondage;**
>
> **And I delivered you out of the hand of the Egyptians, and out of the hand of all that oppressed you, and drave them out from before you, and gave you their land;**
>
> **And I said unto you, I am the Lord your God; fear not the gods of the Amorites, in whose land ye dwell: but ye have not obeyed my voice [Jud. 6:7–10].**

Here goes Israel again, whining and complaining. But God is gracious and good. A prophet came and told them why they were in their present condition. They cried out to God, and God in mercy sent them another judge.

GIDEON, THE SIXTH JUDGE

Now at this juncture, God appeared to Gideon in a most embarrassing situation. We are told:

> **And there came an angel of the Lord, and sat under an oak which was in Ophrah, that pertained unto Joash the**

Abiezrite: and his son Gideon threshed wheat by the winepress, to hide it from the Midianites [Jud. 6:11].

Gideon is not introduced to us as a hero or an outstanding man. Do you know what he is doing? He is threshing wheat by the winepress. Now the winepress is the key to this entire situation. You see, in that day the winepress was always put at the foot of the hill because they brought the grapes down from the vineyard. Naturally, they would carry the heavy grapes downhill; they carried them to the lowest place. In contrast, the threshing floor was always put up on the top of the hill, the highest hill that was available, in order to catch the wind which would drive the chaff away. Here we find Gideon, down at the bottom of the hill, threshing. Now that would be the place to take the grapes, but that is no place to take your crop in order to do your threshing. Can you see the frustration of this man? Why doesn't he go to the hilltop? Well, he is afraid of the Midianites. He does not want them to see that he is threshing wheat. And you can imagine his frustration. There is no air getting to him down there, certainly no wind. So he pitches the grain up into the air. And what happens? Does the chaff blow away? No. It comes down around his neck and gets into his clothes making him very uncomfortable. There he is, trying his best to thresh in a place like that, and all the time rebuking himself for being a coward, afraid to go to the hilltop. I think he looked up there rather longingly and thought, "Do I dare go to the hilltop?" Gideon was having a very frustrating experience, but God was going to use this man. We will see why God used this kind of a man.

It was at that time that the angel of the Lord, which many of us believe was none other than the pre-incarnate Christ, appeared to him. We are told:

And the angel of the LORD appeared unto him, and said unto him, The LORD is with thee, thou mighty man of valour [Jud. 6:12].

Don't tell me, friend, that there is no humor in the Bible. Don't you think it sounds humorous to call Gideon a mighty man of valour? God has a wonderful sense of humor. The Bible is a serious book, of course. It deals with a race that is in sin, and it concerns God's salvation for that race. It reveals God as high and holy and lifted up. But God has a sense of humor and, if you miss that in the Bible, you will not find it nearly as interesting.

Jesus Christ has a great sense of humor. One day He said to the Pharisees, "Ye blind guides, which strain at a gnat, and swallow a camel" (Matt. 23:24). If you don't think that is funny, the next time you see a camel, look at it. A camel has more projections on it than some of our space vehicles. I rode a camel in Egypt and found out they even have horns. They also have the biggest Adam's apple in the world. They have pads on their knees, great big hoofs, and some have one hump, and some have two humps. Everywhere you look at them there is a projection. Can't you see these religious rulers trying to swallow camels? God indeed has a sense of humor.

One of the funniest things the Lord could have called Gideon was a mighty man of valour because he was actually a coward. I think that when Gideon looked up and saw Him and heard Him say, "Thou mighty man of valour," he looked behind him to see if there wasn't somebody else there, because that term did not apply to him. And then he turned to the angel and said, "Who? Me? Do you mean to call me a mighty man of valour when I am down here at the winepress pitching grain up into the air when I ought to be up yonder on top of the hill? If I were a mighty man of valour, that is where I would be, not down here. I am nothing in the world but a coward." The Lord does want to encourage him, of course, but the point is that it was a rather humorous title that the Lord gave to this man.

Well, God has called him now to this office to deliver his people, and He has called a most unusual man. This man is suffering from an inferiority complex.

> **And Gideon said unto him, Oh my Lord, if the LORD be with us, why then is all this befallen us? and where be all his miracles which our fathers told us of, saying, Did not the LORD bring us up from Egypt? but now the LORD**

**hath forsaken us, and delivered us into the hands of the
Midianites [Jud. 6:13].**

Now the angel of the Lord did not say that He was with *Israel* at this
time; He was with Gideon. Frankly, He was not with Israel because of
their sin. The angel said, "The Lord is with *thee*"—singular—with
you, Gideon. But Gideon cannot believe that God would be with him.
He wants to know where all those miracles are that their fathers had
told them about. He believed that the Lord had forsaken Israel. He was
as wrong as a man could be. The Lord had not really forsaken them;
they had forsaken the Lord.

This man is in a bad state mentally and a bad state spiritually. Actually, he not only had an inferiority complex, he was skeptical, he was
cynical, he was weak, and he was cowardly. That is this man Gideon.
What a wrong impression is given of him today when he is described
as a knight in shining armor, a Sir Lancelot, or a Sir Galahad. Why, he
was nothing in the world but a Don Quixote charging a windmill, my
beloved. He was the biggest coward that you have ever seen. But this
was the man that God called.

**And the Lord looked upon him, and said, Go in this thy
might, and thou shalt save Israel from the hand of the
Midianites: have not I sent thee? [Jud. 6:14].**

This is the call and commission of Gideon. It is a commission of courage. It is interesting to note, however, that even at this point Gideon did
not believe God. Note what Gideon says:

**And he said unto him, Oh my Lord, wherewith shall I
save Israel? behold, my family is poor in Manasseh, and
I am the least in my father's house [Jud. 6:15].**

Now consider for a moment the position Gideon occupies in his own
thinking. He said in effect, "You certainly are not asking me to do this.
To begin with, I belong to the nation Israel. We are now under the heel
of the Midianites." It was bad enough to be under Egypt, but imagine

being under these nomads of the desert, the Midianites! "We are in slavery. Here we are hiding, and here I am threshing at the foot of the hill. And you come and call me? Well, to begin with, the tribe of Manasseh (one of the sons of Joseph) is not noted for anything; we have had no conspicuous men. In the tribe of Manasseh, my family is not very well known. We are sort of ne'er-do-wells. We are not prominent folk. In my family I happen to be the very least one. You made a big mistake in calling me because you happen to have called the smallest pebble that is on the beach." Honestly, this man felt that he was the last man in Israel to be used of God. And do you know that he was right? He was the last man in Israel that God should have called.

Our problem today, friend, is that most of us are too strong for God to use. Most of us are too capable for God to use. You notice that God only uses weak men, don't you? First Corinthians 1:26–27 tells us that this is so: "For ye see your calling, brethren, how that not many wise men after the flesh, not many mighty, not many noble, are called: But God hath chosen the foolish things of the world to confound the wise; and God hath chosen the weak things of the world to confound the things which are mighty." God used all of these judges but not because they were capable or outstanding. Does that encourage you, friend? Do you know why God does not use most of us? We are too strong. Most of us have too much talent for God to use us. Most of us today are doing our own will and going our own way. There are multitudes of people, talented people, people with ability, whom God is not using. Do you know why? They are too strong for God to use. Paul mentions this: "And base things of the world, and things which are despised, hath God chosen, yea, and things which are not, to bring to nought things that are: That no flesh should glory in his presence" (1 Cor. 1:28–29). There is something wrong with any Christian worker who is proud. God does not use the flesh. Anything that this poor preacher does in the weakness of the flesh and boasts about is despised by God. God hates it and cannot use it. God wants weak vessels and that is the only kind he will use. God follows this policy so that no flesh will glory in His presence. When God gets ready to do anything, He chooses the weakest thing He can get in order to make it clear that He is doing it, not the weak arm of the flesh. That is God's method.

Remember Moses down in the bulrushes was only a little baby. Then look at Pharaoh Ramses II, the strongest of the pharaohs, who sat on the throne. He is the one who built the great cities of Egypt. Put the one down by the side of the other—the little weak, helpless baby and the powerful Pharaoh on the throne—and whom will you take? Of course you would take the Pharaoh because he is the strong one. But God took the little fellow in the bulrushes to demonstrate that He uses the weak things of the world to confound the wise.

Also God chose a man by the name of Elijah. Elijah was not a weak man, but he had to become weak. God had to put that man through a series of tests. He schooled him in the desert and finally forced him to listen to the still, small voice of God. And Elijah did not much care for still, small voices. This is the man who liked the three-ring circus, the fireworks, the noise and the fanfare, but God had to train him and let him know that He chooses the weak things of the world. After Elijah walked into the court of Ahab and Jezebel, he told them it would not rain for several years. Then God put him out by the brook Cherith. There as he saw the brook dry up, he found out that his life was no more than a dried-up brook. Later he looked down into an empty flour barrel, but he could sing the doxology. When he did, God fed him and the widow's family out of that empty flour barrel. Why? Because God chooses and uses weak things.

Then consider Simon Peter. Whoever would have chosen him? Why, everybody knew he was as weak as water, and our Lord said, "You are going to be a rock-man. I will make you as stable as a rock." I imagine everybody laughed when He said that. Even Simon Peter gave up on one occasion and said, "Depart from me; for I am a sinful man" (Luke 5:8). What he is really saying is this, "Why don't you give me up and go get somebody else? I am such a failure." But the Lord Jesus said, "Fear not; from henceforth thou shalt catch men" (Luke 5:10). In effect He said, "You are the very one I want. You are going to preach the first sermon on the day of Pentecost which will bring three thousand people to Me. I am going to demonstrate that I can use the weakest thing in the world." God always does that, my beloved. The interesting thing is, someone has said, that Nero was on the throne while Paul was being beheaded. At first glance, it looked like Paul had lost and Nero had won. But history had already handed down its decision. Men name their sons Paul and call their dogs Nero. This is quite interesting, is it not? God is choosing the weak things of this world.

Have you ever compared that little Baby in Bethlehem with Caesar Augustus who could sign a tax bill and the whole civilized world was taxed? Which would you pick? I would take the tax-gatherer every time because he seems to have a lot of power, but God took that little Baby in Bethlehem, for He was His Son. God always chooses that way.

Although Gideon was a very weak individual, God told him that he was the one who was going to deliver Israel. Yes, God is going to use Gideon, but first He must train him. Gideon had to overcome his fear and develop courage. He needed faith to help strengthen his feeble knees and make him patient. I want you to notice some of the training that he went through. He immediately, you see, was afraid; so God gave him his first lesson.

And the LORD said unto him, Peace be unto thee; fear not: thou shalt not die [Jud. 6:23].

He said, "Thou shalt not die," because Gideon feared that he would die after seeing God. And he told Gideon to go to his own hometown, to begin there by throwing over the altar of Baal, and burning the grove that was by it. All of this represented the worst sort of immorality.

GIDEON REPUDIATES BAAL: ISRAEL
CALLED TO ARMS

Then Gideon built an altar there unto the LORD, and called it Jehovah-shalom: unto this day it is yet in Ophrah of the Abiezrites.

And it came to pass the same night, that the LORD said unto him, Take thy father's young bullock, even the second bullock of seven years old, and throw down the altar of Baal that thy father hath, and cut down the grove that is by it:

And build an altar unto the LORD thy God upon the top of this rock, in the ordered place, and take the second bullock, and offer a burnt sacrifice with the wood of the grove which thou shalt cut down.

Then Gideon took ten men of his servants, and did as the LORD had said unto him: and so it was, because he feared his father's household, and the men of the city, that he could not do it by day, that he did it by night [Jud. 6:24–27].

And so Gideon begins his adventure. Even with God's commission he is still afraid. Instead of obeying God in the bold daylight, he does it under the cover of darkness. But they find out who did it, and they are ready to execute Gideon. But God again delivers him.

Gideon is still hesitant. God has to overcome the fear. God has to develop courage and faith. God has to strengthen Gideon's feeble knees. It is a patient, long ordeal. The next step is to fill this man with His Spirit—God has always given a filling of the Spirit to the man that He uses.

But the spirit of the LORD came upon Gideon, and he blew a trumpet; and Abiezer was gathered after him [Jud. 6:34].

The blowing of the trumpet meant war. The minute he blew the trumpet, his people knew it meant war against the Amalekites, and they began to gather unto him.

Do you know what happened? Gideon got cold feet and went back to the Lord with a proposition.

And Gideon said unto God, If thou wilt save Israel by mine hand, as thou hast said,

Behold, I will put a fleece of wool in the floor; and if the dew be on the fleece only, and it be dry upon all the earth beside, then shall I know that thou wilt save Israel by mine hand, as thou hast said.

And it was so: for he rose up early on the morrow, and thrust the fleece together, and wringed the dew out of the fleece, a bowl full of water [Jud. 6:36–38].

The next day Gideon went back (and I am of the opinion that he intended to do this all the time regardless of the outcome of the first test because if you put out a fleece here in California it would be damp, whereas the ground would be dry). He gave a two-way test that could not be gainsaid. He said, "Now, Lord, I will put out the fleece again. If You are really in this thing, put the dew around everywhere else and let the fleece remain dry." I am glad he did it that way because, frankly, I would be skeptical enough to believe it "just happened" the first time. Or let us say that it was natural for it to happen one way, but it was supernatural for it to happen the other way. This man asked God to put dew on the fleece and then for God not to put dew on the fleece. How gracious God was to Gideon. We will find that God will gradually school this man until He brings him to the place where Gideon can see that there is nothing in him. Then God will use him to win a mighty battle.

Now, looking back at verses 34 and 35, we see that men for his army had come to him from everywhere. When a trumpet is blown in Israel, it means war. And frankly, friend, he was the last man you would want to gather around. He certainly was not a man prepared to lead them into battle. So God begins to move in this man's life in a definite way, as we shall see in chapter 7.

THREE HUNDRED ALERT SOLDIERS ARE CHOSEN

Then Jerubbaal, who is Gideon, and all the people that were with him, rose up early, and pitched beside the well of Harod: so that the host of the Midianites were on the north side of them, by the hill of Moreh, in the valley.

> And the LORD said unto Gideon, The people that are
> with thee are too many for me to give the Midianites into
> their hands, lest Israel vaunt themselves against me,
> saying, Mine own hand hath saved me [Jud. 7:1–2].

Now Gideon goes out and looks at his army. He had thirty-two thousand men, and the thought in Gideon's mind is that this is not enough. The Midianites were like grasshoppers on the hills. They were disorganized, but by sheer numbers they would have overcome the Israelites. Therefore, his men were too few, and I think Gideon was ready to blow the trumpet again. But God said to Gideon, "You have too many men. I cannot give you the victory with thirty-two thousand men because you would boast and say that you did it in your own strength, power, and might." No flesh is going to glory in God's presence. That is the reason God has to use weak instruments today. This is the method He continues to follow. He is going to cut down the number of the army.

> Now therefore go to, proclaim in the ears of the people,
> saying, Whosoever is fearful and afraid, let him return
> and depart early from mount Gilead. And there re-
> turned of the people twenty and two thousand; and
> there remained ten thousand [Jud. 7:3].

Gideon had thirty-two thousand men and now he has lost twenty-two thousand of them! You may recall God's condition, as put down in the Mosaic system in the Book of Deuteronomy that if anyone was drafted into the army and was *afraid*, he could go home.

I have often wondered why Gideon did not go home. When he said, "All of you who are fearful and afraid," he could have said, "Follow me, because I am going home, I am more afraid than anyone here." He had to stay, however. God had commissioned him.

Now Gideon has only ten thousand men, and that is enough to make anyone afraid. But God says, "Really, you still have too many men. You have to reduce this number. I cannot give you victory with this number of men in your army." So Gideon and his men went through another test.

> **So he brought down the people unto the water: and the Lord said unto Gideon, Every one that lappeth of the water with his tongue, as a dog lappeth, him shalt thou set by himself; likewise every one that boweth down upon his knees to drink.**
>
> **And the number of them that lapped, putting their hand to their mouth, were three hundred men: but all the rest of the people bowed down upon their knees to drink water.**
>
> **And the Lord said unto Gideon, By the three hundred men that lapped will I save you, and deliver the Midianites into thine hand: and let all the other people go every man unto his place [Jud. 7:5–7].**

Do you know what we have here? It is one of the finest lessons concerning divine election and man's free will. This is the way they work together. God said to Gideon, "I am going to choose the men that I want to go with you, but the way I will do it is to let them make the choice. Bring them down to the water, and the ones who lap water like a dog, just going through and throwing it into their mouths, are the ones I have chosen. You can put aside those men who get down on all fours and take their time drinking. I don't want them."

Had we been there (ours is a great day for interviewing the man on the street), we could have had interviews with the men in Gideon's army. For example, let us take the man that is down on all fours. We would go up to him and say, "Brother, why did you get down on all fours?" "Well," he would reply, "I was just wondering why I didn't go home with the other crowd. I have been thinking this thing over and I have a wife and family, and I just do not think I ought to be here. I feel like I should have gone home. I have no heart for this." He made his choice, but God also made His choice. That is divine election and human free will. You see, God elects, but He lets you be the one to make the choice. Then we go to the man that lapped water like a dog, and went to the other side of the stream. "Why did you lap water like that?" we ask him. He says, "Where are the Midianites?" "Wait just a minute," we reply. "Why did you do that?" He replies, "Because I am with Gideon one hundred percent!" May I say to you that these three hundred men had a heart for battle. If you had said to any one of these three hundred men, "Say, did you know that God has elected you?" he would have replied, "I don't know what you are talking about. The thing is that I want to go after these Midianites!"

You can argue about divine election and free will all you want to, but it works. You cannot make it work out by arguing, but it sure works out in life, friend. Each one of the ten thousand men in Gideon's army exercised his free will. God did not interfere with one of them as far as their free wills were concerned. Today God, through His Son Jesus Christ, offers you the free gift of salvation. It is a legitimate offer. It is a sincere offer from God Himself. He says, "All that the Father giveth me shall come to me; and him that cometh to me I will in no wise cast out" (John 6:37). Now don't tell me that you can argue about election right now. You cannot. You can come to God if you want to come. If you don't come, I have news for you—you were not elected. If you do come, I have good news for you—you were elected. That is the way God moves.

Now these three hundred men often have been misunderstood. As a student, I went down to a little church in Georgia. When I got there, a dear little lady wearing a sunbonnet said to me, "Mr. McGee, we have here just a little Gideon's band." They didn't have a Gideon's band! They had the most discouraged, lazy folk I have ever seen in my life. That is not Gideon's band. Gideon's band was a group of dedicated men, willing to die to deliver Israel, men who had their hearts and souls in this matter. May I say to you that these men lapped up water like a dog because they were after the Midianites and not after water. They will drink after the battle is over.

I once watched a football game, and then I listened to the interview of the quarterback of the Arkansas team. Even after the game, he was so excited and so emotional that he took no credit for winning. He said, "We were determined to win." That is Gideon's band, friend, and that is the thing that is needed today in the church, if you please.

ISRAEL'S VICTORY OVER MIDIAN

But if thou fear to go down, go thou with Phurah thy servant down to the host:

And thou shalt hear what they say; and afterward shall thine hands be strengthened to go down unto the host. Then went he down with Phurah his servant unto the outside of the armed men that were in the host.

And the Midianites and the Amalekites and all the children of the east lay along in the valley like grasshoppers for multitude; and their camels were without number, as the sand by the sea side for multitude.

And when Gideon was come, behold, there was a man that told a dream unto his fellow, and said, Behold, I dreamed a dream, and, lo, a cake of barley bread tumbled into the host of Midian, and came unto a tent, and smote it that it fell, and overturned it, that the tent lay along.

And his fellow answered and said, This is nothing else save the sword of Gideon the son of Joash, a man of Israel: for into his hand hath God delivered Midian, and all the host [Jud. 7:10–14].

This is Gideon's final lesson before he goes into battle. He goes down to the edge of the camp and eavesdrops while two soldiers are talking. They frankly believe that God is going to deliver the Midianites into the hands of Gideon and his host. God permits Gideon to hear this conversation to encourage him just prior to battle.

And he divided the three hundred men into three companies, and he put a trumpet in every man's hand, with empty pitchers, and lamps within the pitchers.

And he said unto them, Look on me, and do likewise: and, behold, when I come to the outside of the camp, it shall be that, as I do, so shall ye do.

When I blow with a trumpet, I and all that are with me, then blow ye the trumpets also on every side of all the camp, and say, The sword of the LORD, and of Gideon.

So Gideon, and the hundred men that were with him, came unto the outside of the camp in the beginning of the middle watch; and they had but newly set the watch: and they blew the trumpets, and brake the pitchers that were in their hands.

And the three companies blew the trumpets, and brake the pitchers, and held the lamps in their left hands, and the trumpets in their right hands to blow withal: and they cried, The sword of the LORD, and of Gideon.

And they stood every man in his place round about the camp: and all the host ran, and cried, and fled.

And the three hundred blew the trumpets, and the LORD set every man's sword against his fellow, even throughout all the host: and the host fled to Beth-shittah in Zererath, and to the border of Abel-meholah, unto Tabbath [Jud. 7:16–22].

This is the record given of Gideon's strategy. He divides his three hundred men into three groups. They are given three things: pitchers, lamps, and trumpets. The lamps were put inside the pitchers so that the light could not be seen, and they held them in one hand and their trumpets they held in the other hand. When they went into battle, their cry was to be, "The sword of the Lord and of Gideon." The interesting thing is that Gideon did not have a sword and neither did any of the three hundred men. You see they were under the rule of the Midianites, and the Midianites did not let them have an arsenal. They kept the weapons and the swords for themselves. So Gideon's strategy employed pitchers, lamps, and trumpets.

As we have said before, the Midianites and Amalekites were among the nomadic tribes of the desert. They had raided the land of Israel and seized their crops and supplies. They had a very loose organization. They moved as disorganized nomads through the desert and did not have an organized army. They had set a few guards about the camp but most of the people were asleep, here, there, and yonder. They did not expect to be attacked at night. To begin with, it is difficult to see at night. So Gideon posted his three hundred men in three groups around the camp. At a certain time they blew their trumpets and broke the pitchers so that the light shone out. Each trumpet represented the fact that there were probably several hundred of the enemy present. Imagine the Midianites waking out of a sound sleep. The first thing they did was start whacking their swords in every direction. The Israelites did not have swords. All they did was hold the light so the Midianites could go after each other. It was a regular riot! The Midianites soon fled over the hills into the tall timber and out of the area. This gave Gideon and the Israelites a tremendous victory.

There are some wonderful spiritual lessons in this account. First of all, I would like to go back to this matter of the dew on the fleece. We need God today to do an interior decorating job on our lives. We need to ask Him for dew on our barren lives. In Hosea 14:5 God says, "I will be as the dew unto Israel: he shall grow as the lily, and cast forth his roots as Lebanon." God speaks about this subject several times. "And of Joseph he said, Blessed of the LORD be his land, for the precious things of heaven, for the dew, and for the deep that coucheth beneath" (Deut. 33:13). "The king's wrath is as the roaring of a lion; but his favour is as dew upon the grass" (Prov. 19:12). "By his knowledge the depths are broken up, and the clouds drop down the dew" (Prov. 3:20). Finally, in Psalm 133:1–3, God says, "Behold, how good and how pleasant it is for brethren to dwell together in unity! It is like the precious ointment upon the head, that ran down upon the beard, even Aaron's beard: that went down to the skirts of his garments; As the dew of Hermon, and as the dew that descended upon the mountains of Zion: for there the LORD commanded the blessing, even life for evermore." God has blessed in this way. We need that touch—that fresh touch. We need it like dew upon the rosebud and the grass in the morning. We need a tender touch.

Hosea 14:5 tells us that the lily is delicate. He, our Lord God, will come down upon us like rain upon the mown grass. Even when we are in trouble, and He has cut us down, He will come down upon us like rain. Our Lord could weep over Jerusalem, but do we weep today over sinners? The Publican could smite his breast and cry out about his sin, but what about us today? We need a touch from God that will make us strong and stable, grounded and settled. Oh that we could say with the psalmist, "My heart is fixed, O God, my heart is fixed: I will sing and give praise" (Ps. 57:7).

We need the dew of God upon our lives to bring purity into our lives. Peter tells us in 2 Peter 3:14, "Wherefore, beloved, seeing that ye look for such things, be diligent that ye may be found of him in peace, without spot, and blameless." This is what we need today. God only uses a clean cup. 1 Peter 1:16 says, "Because it is written, Be ye holy; for I am holy." God says this to us. "Having therefore these promises, dearly beloved, let us cleanse ourselves from all filthiness of the flesh and spirit, perfecting holiness in the fear of God" (2 Cor. 7:1). What a wonderful picture and lesson we have here.

Now let us look at another spiritual lesson concerning the pitchers. "But we have this treasure in earthen vessels . . ." (2 Cor. 4:7). Those pitchers represent the bodies of believers. That is what Paul means when he says, "I beseech you therefore, brethren, by the mercies of God, that ye present your bodies [your total personalities] a living sacrifice . . . unto God . . ." (Rom. 12:1). That is the reason we ought not to glory in any man. Paul says that. "Therefore let no man glory in men . . ." (1 Cor. 3:21). That is the earthen vessel. We have this treasure in earthen vessels—pitchers. Some of us are not broken and, as a result, the light does not shine through. It is not our light that we should shine, but the light of the Lord Jesus Christ. His light should shine through us. It can only shine in a broken life. We are to shine as lights in the world. Paul told the Philippians, "Do all things without murmurings and disputings: That ye may be blameless and harmless, the sons of God, without rebuke, in the midst of a crooked and perverse nation, among whom ye shine as lights in the world" (Phil. 2:14–15).

Let's look for a moment at the trumpets. First Corinthians 14:8 says, "For if the trumpet give an uncertain sound, who shall prepare himself to the battle?" This speaks of the testimony and witness of believers. The testimony and witness of believers must be certain and clear.

FORTY YEARS OF PEACE UNDER GIDEON

Chapter 8 is a continuance of the record of Gideon, the judge. Here you find events that came to pass after the remarkable deliverance that God gave Gideon over the Midianites. The children of Israel are free again and, as a result, they are prosperous. Zebah and Zalmunna, Midianite kings, have been pursued and slain. The Israelites are being blessed for the first time in a long time, and they are so grateful to Gideon for all that he has done that they want him to rule over them.

> **Then the men of Israel said unto Gideon, Rule thou over us, both thou, and thy son, and thy son's son also: for thou hast delivered us from the hand of Midian [Jud. 8:22].**

This is the first indication given to us in Scripture that the children of Israel wanted a king to rule over them. God told them at the beginning that He did not want them to have a king like the nations round about them. But because Gideon had delivered them from bondage, they wanted him to accept the position of king. He apparently is the first one to have been offered this high position, and he turned it down. Later on we will discover that Israel asks for a king again. In fact, they insist upon having a king, and finally they demand one. Then God tells Samuel (who is the last of the judges and the first in the line of the prophets) that he is to anoint a king for them. Also God makes it clear that Israel is not rejecting Samuel, but is rejecting God. God wanted to rule over His people. The form of government for Israel was to be a theocracy. In this case, it was God who had used Gideon so remarkably, but it is Gideon whom Israel wants to rule over them. They not only want Gideon to rule, but his son and his son's son also. This means that they want a king like the nations around them.

Notice the remarkable answer that Gideon gave the people.

And Gideon said unto them, I will not rule over you, neither shall my son rule over you: the LORD shall rule over you [Jud. 8:23].

Gideon certainly had learned a lesson; there is no question about it. This young man who threshed grain down by the winepress, recognized that he was a coward. He knew that it was God who had given him the victory. He knew he had no strength in himself to win the battle, but he realized God had raised him up for this purpose. Gideon was indeed a remarkable person. He is mentioned in Hebrews chapter 11 where the "Heroes of the Faith" are listed. In fact, he leads the list of judges. He is also ahead of David in the list. "And what shall I more say? for the time would fail me to tell of Gedeon, and of Barak, and of Samson, and of Jephthae; of David also, and Samuel, and of the prophets: Who through faith subdued kingdoms, wrought righteousness, obtained promises, stopped the mouths of lions, Quenched the violence of fire, escaped the edge of the sword, out of weakness were made strong, waxed valiant in fight, turned to flight the armies of the aliens" (Heb. 11:32–34). The writer of Hebrews says that time would fail to tell everything about these men, and he wanted to tell about Gideon. God raised up Gideon to perform an extraordinary task. It teaches us that any man or woman that God uses has to be used on God's terms. And He chooses the weak things of this world.

It seems as though each judge had some glaring weakness and in most cases God used it. Gideon's weakness was the fact that he was a coward. At times I have felt very close to this man in my ministry. When I became pastor of the great Church of the Open Door in Los Angeles, California, in 1949, I preached my first message on Gideon. I put myself in his class. I came to that congregation in weakness. The only reason I could see that God called me was because I was like

Gideon—weak and cowardly. I have rejoiced in the fact that God did for me what He did for Gideon. God certainly was with me, and I have always been grateful to Him. I have discovered that when I get in the way (and I do sometimes), then I stumble and fall. But as long as I am willing to let God have His way, it is remarkable what He will do. I give God all of the glory for my radio ministry, friend. I never sought it. I did not start out after it. Like Topsy, it "just growed." God has blessed it, and I rejoice in it. He has been wonderful.

I wish we could end the story of Gideon here, but he had another weakness.

And Gideon had threescore and ten sons of his body begotten: for he had many wives.

And his concubine that was in Shechem, she also bare him a son, whose name he called Abimelech [Jud. 8:30–31].

Gideon had many wives and a concubine besides. He had a total of seventy-one sons. That is a real blot on this man's life. Now someone will say, as they did about Solomon, *"How* could God use a man like this and *why* did He use him?" Well, Gideon took these many wives and had all these children after the battle. And the fact of the matter is that God used him in spite of this. God did not approve of what he did. The record makes it clear that his actions brought tragedy to the nation of Israel. The next chapter brings that out. God had forbidden intermarriage outside the nation. He had forbidden the Israelites to have more than one wife. God did not create several Eves for Adam. He created only one. God did not remove all of Adam's ribs. God took out only one rib.

Abraham, you remember, took a concubine, that little Egyptian maid named Hagar and, believe me, it caused trouble, God never sanctioned it. Through Abraham's son Isaac came the nation Israel. The Arabs are descendants of Ishmael, Abraham's son by Hagar. I talked to an Arab guide in Jericho who was very proud of the fact that he was a son of Abraham. He was also a Moslem. He said proudly, "I am a son of Abraham through Ishmael." That is true. That was the sin of Abraham, and God never blessed that, friend. God did not bless Solomon's actions in this connection, and He is not going to bless Gideon either. In fact, Gideon's actions split the kingdom and caused real tragedy. This is the blot in his life. God does not hide anything. God paints the picture of man as it is. Now if a friend of Gideon had been his biographer, he probably would have left this part of his life out of the story. God, however, did not. He paints mankind in all of his lurid, sinful color.

CONFUSION AFTER GIDEON'S DEATH

And it came to pass, as soon as Gideon was dead, that the children of Israel turned again, and went a whoring after Baalim, and made Baal-berith their god.

And the children of Israel remembered not the LORD their God, who had delivered them out of the hands of all their enemies on every side:

Neither shewed they kindness to the house of Jerubbaal, namely, Gideon, according to all the goodness which he had shewed unto Israel [Jud. 8:33–35].

This is the same old story, is it not? The hoop of history continues to roll as it is rolling today. At first they were a nation who served God, then they did evil, forsook God, turned to Baal, and God sells them into slavery and servitude. Then they cry out to God. Then they repent, and God raises up a judge to deliver them. Here goes Israel again. As soon as Gideon was dead, the children of Israel, turned from God and went a whoring after Baalim. That is the sad, sordid story of Israel, and also the story of His church today. This up and down business is the story of nations, churches, and individuals. Today many of us are just rolling a hoop through this world. One day we are up, and the next day we are down. God never intended our spiritual lives to be that way.

CHAPTERS 9 AND 10

THEME: Fifth apostasy; Abimelech responsible for civil war

THE CAREER OF ABIMELECH, GIDEON'S SON

This chapter records the story of Abimelech, the sinful and wicked son of Gideon and his concubine. You see, Gideon should not have had a concubine. It certainly caused trouble in the nation.

> And Abimelech the son of Jerubbaal went to Shechem unto his mother's brethren, and communed with them, and with all the family of the house of his mother's father, saying,
>
> Speak, I pray you, in the ears of all the men of Shechem, Whether is better for you, either that all the sons of Jerubbaal, which are three score and ten persons, reign over you, or that one reign over you? remember also that I am your bone and your flesh.
>
> And his mother's brethren spake of him in the ears of all the men of Shechem all these words: and their hearts inclined to follow Abimelech; for they said, He is our brother [Jud. 9:1–3].

This boy Abimelech is very ambitious. He had heard about the nation wanting Gideon to become ruler over them. Since he is a son of Gideon, he wants to become king. So he goes to his mother's people, who are in Shechem, and gets them to follow him.

> And he went unto his father's house at Ophrah, and slew his brethren the sons of Jerubbaal, being threescore and ten persons, upon one stone: notwithstanding yet Jo-

tham the youngest son of Jerubbaal was left; for he hid himself [Jud. 9:5].

Obviously, Abimelech is a wicked and brutal man. He does a horrible thing here.

Some Bible expositors rate Abimelech as a judge. He may have been a judge, at least it is said that he "reigned three years over Israel." Dr. James M. Gray wrote, "The usurped rule of Abimelech, the fratricide, is not usually counted [as a judge]." He brutally murdered the seventy sons of Gideon and set himself up as king. His abortive reign reveals, I feel, the truth of the statement in Daniel: ". . . the most High ruleth in the kingdom of men, and giveth it to whomsoever he will, and setteth up over it the basest of men" (Dan. 4:17). Even today when a good ruler comes into office, many folk say, "God raised him up." What about the wicked ruler? God permits him to come to the throne also. Do you know why? Because the principle is "like priest, like people." That is, people get the ruler they deserve. The people of Israel wanted this boy Abimelech to rule over them; and they got the caliber of man they deserved. Friend, when we look around our world today, we find this principle is still true.

Now we find that God judges Abimelech for the awful thing he did, and He also judges the men of Shechem for making him king and starting him out on such a course. Civil war ensued because there were many people who did not want Abimelech, of course.

And Abimelech came unto the tower, and fought against it, and went hard unto the door of the tower to burn it with fire.

And a certain woman cast a piece of a millstone upon Abimelech's head, and all to brake his skull.

Then he called hastily unto the young man his armour-bearer, and said unto him, Draw thy sword, and slay me, that men say not of me, A woman slew him. And his young man thrust him through, and he died.

And when the men of Israel saw that Abimelech was dead, they departed every man unto his place.

Thus God rendered the wickedness of Abimelech, which he did unto his father, in slaying his seventy brethren:

And all the evil of the men of Shechem did God render upon their heads: and upon them came the curse of Jotham the son of Jerubbaal [Jud. 9:52–57].

This is a sad ending for the life of Gideon who fathered this illegitimate son, Abimelech. God lifted Gideon from a very humble position to be the deliverer and judge of His people. How sad that a man who accomplished so much good should allow this in his life of which God did not approve and which resulted in civil war in Israel.

TOLA, THE SEVENTH JUDGE

Tola and Jair become the next judges. Maybe you have never heard of Tola. If you haven't, it is perfectly all right. He did nothing noteworthy.

And after Abimelech there arose to defend Israel Tola the son of Puah, the son of Dodo, a man of Issachar, and he dwelt in Shamir in mount Ephraim.

And he judged Israel twenty and three years, and died, and was buried in Shamir [Jud. 10:1–2].

What did Tola do? He died and was buried in Shamir. Not one thing is recorded about any achievements. Although he was a judge in Israel twenty-three years, there is not one thing that can be mentioned about the deeds of this man, from the day he was born to the day he died. All you have here is what is on his tombstone: "Born—died."

JAIR, THE EIGHTH JUDGE

And after him arose Jair, a Gileadite, and judged Israel twenty and two years.

And he had thirty sons that rode on thirty ass colts, and they had thirty cities, which are called Havoth-jair unto this day, which are in the land of Gilead.

And Jair died, and was buried in Camon [Jud. 10:3–5].

All that we are told about this man is that he had thirty sons and he bought each one of them a little donkey. He did not get them a Jaguar, Mustang, Pinto, or Cougar, he gave each boy a donkey. What a sight it must have been to see these thirty boys ride out of Gilead!

In Jair's story I can see three things: (1) prosperity without purpose; (2) affluence without influence; (3) prestige without power.

In that day a donkey was a mark of prosperity. That was the thing that denoted a man's wealth. For example, Judges 5:10 says, "Speak, ye that ride on white asses, ye that sit in judgment, and walk by the way." This verse speaks about the upper echelon, or the establishment. The donkey was a mark of wealth and was the animal that kings rode upon. There has always been a question about whether or not they had horses in that day. In Scripture the little donkey is the animal of peace and the horse is the animal of war (the horse was imported into that land). But the little donkey was actually the mark of prosperity and the mark of a king.

You remember that the Lord Jesus Christ rode into Jerusalem on a little donkey. We misinterpret Zechariah 9:9 which says, "Rejoice greatly, O daughter of Zion; shout, O daughter of Jerusalem: behold, thy King cometh unto thee: he is just, and having salvation; lowly, and riding upon an ass, and upon a colt the foal of an ass." Zechariah does not mean that the Lord Jesus is humble because He is riding on a little donkey. He is humble in spite of the fact that He is riding upon an animal which only kings ride. If He had not been King, it would really have been a presumption to ride into Jerusalem on that donkey as He did and receive all of the adulation and hosannas from the crowd that day.

Jair was obviously a man of wealth and prominence to be able to afford thirty donkeys. He gave each one of his sons a donkey, so he must have had a thirty-car garage! This was the mark of a benevolent father. He was generous, and I think he spoiled his sons. He got them what they wanted. They lived in the lap of luxury and with golden spoons in their mouths. Donkeys probably came in several models, and Jair bought each son the latest thing. But did these donkeys bring glory to God? Did they make Jair a better judge? Did they bring blessing to the people? Did any one of these boys go out as a missionary? No. They lived in Gilead.

It is true that there is nothing particularly wrong with donkeys. On the other hand, there is nothing particularly right with a man who is a judge and spends a whole lot of time with many boys and donkeys. This is important for us to see. Our Lord rode into Jerusalem on a little donkey to fulfill prophecy and to present Himself as King, and the hosannas were sung. Satan was angry and the religious rulers protested as Christ rode through the gate and into the city. But all of Jair's donkeys never lifted one hosanna. When these animals brayed, I think Satan smiled and the mob was entertained. Jair is a picture of prosperity without purpose, friend, and it is a dangerous thing. We see the same picture in the days of Noah when they were marrying and giving in marriage. This is also demonstrated in the account of Solomon sending out ships to bring back apes and peacocks—peacocks for beauty and apes for entertainment.

Years ago a high school class in the state of Washington came up with this motto for their graduating class: "Pep without purpose is piffle." Well, it is not much of a motto, but it certainly expresses present-day conditions. We have prosperity but without purpose. May I ask you what the goal of your life is? Is it pointless? Is it aimless? Have you found life pretty boring? Shakespeare's Hamlet said, "How stale, flat and unprofitable seem to me the uses of this world." What we need today is direction and dimension in our lives. We need a cause, and the cause of Jesus Christ is still the greatest challenge any man can have. Old Jair was some judge, wasn't he?

Jair's days were also marked by prestige without power. He was the outstanding man in the community. The traffic cops probably never gave any of his sons a ticket. But verse 5 does not speak of a monument for Jair. He was buried in an unknown spot. He never performed one conspicuous act. He never did a worthwhile deed. He never gained a victory. He may have had thirty donkeys, but he had no spiritual power. We are living in a day when the church has lost its power. What a picture we have in this man Jair.

Right before World War II, the city of Pasadena was having its annual Rose Parade. The float that was entered by the Standard Oil Company was covered with American Beauty roses. It was a sight to behold. The theme of the parade was, "Be prepared." Right in the middle of the parade the Standard Oil Company's float ran out of gas. It stopped right where I was viewing the parade. I couldn't help but laugh. If there was one float that should not have run out of gas, it was that one. Standard Oil Company should have had plenty of gas! As I looked at the float, I saw a picture of many Christians today. They are beautiful, but they have no power in their lives. They have beauty and prestige, but no power. That was judge Jair for you. He did nothing, died, and was buried.

EIGHTEEN YEARS OF SERVITUDE UNDER THE PHILISTINES AND AMMONITES

And the children of Israel did evil again in the sight of the LORD, and served Baalim, and Ashtaroth, and the gods of Syria, and the gods of Zidon, and the gods of Moab, and the gods of the children of Ammon, and the gods of the Philistines, and forsook the LORD, and served not him [Jud. 10:6].

You would think that after all their experiences, the Israelites would learn that when they turned to idolatry, trouble came upon them. Because of their idolatry, they went into slavery again—they served the Philistines and Ammonites for eighteen years. Human nature is fallen nature. Jeremiah has said, "The heart is deceitful above all things, and desperately wicked: who can know it?" (Jer. 17:9). You and I certainly do not know the heart. It is easier for us to point our finger back to these people who lived about one thousand years before Christ and say, "You did wrong," than it is for us to see what we are doing wrong.

How are we doing today, by the way? May I say that there is a frightful apostasy today in the church. Human nature is like that, and we are in a nation that is in trouble. We have tried every method, political scheme, and political party, and none of them has worked. What is wrong? We have gone to the wrong place for help. Only a turning to God will get us on the right path. I know that sounds square and out of date, but it sounded that way one thousand years before Christ also. The Israelites turned to other gods, refused to serve the living God, and look at what happened.

> And the anger of the LORD was hot against Israel, and he sold them into the hands of the Philistines, and into the hands of the children of Ammon [Jud. 10:7].

God can afford to remove His instrument when that instrument fails Him. A great many people think that God has to have the church, even a particular church, and that God has to have America because it is sending out missionaries. May I say to you that God does not have to have any of us. He is not dependent upon us at all. We are, however, dependent upon Him.

Israel was probably at its lowest point at this time. Things were very bad for them.

> And the children of Israel cried unto the LORD, saying, We have sinned against thee, both because we have forsaken our God, and also served Baalim [Jud. 10:10].

These people finally got so desperate that they turned to God. Here we see the same old story being acted out once again. It is the hoop of history that is rolling, and it is still rolling today. So then what happened?

And the Lord said unto the children of Israel, Did not I deliver you from the Egyptians, from the Amorites, from the children of Ammon, and from the Philistines?

The Zidonians also, and the Amalekites, and the Maonites, did oppress you; and ye cried to me, and I delivered you out of their hand.

Yet ye have forsaken me, and served other gods: wherefore I will deliver you no more.

Go and cry unto the gods which ye have chosen; let them deliver you in the time of your tribulation.

And the children of Israel said unto the Lord, We have sinned: do thou unto us whatsoever seemeth good unto thee; deliver us only, we pray thee, this day.

And they put away the strange gods from among them, and served the Lord: and his soul was grieved for the misery of Israel [Jud. 10:11-16].

How merciful and gracious God is!

Then the children of Ammon were gathered together, and encamped in Gilead. And the children of Israel assembled themselves together, and encamped in Mizpeh.

And the people and princes of Gilead said to one another, What man is he that will begin to fight against the children of Ammon? he shall be head over all the inhabitants of Gilead [Jud. 10:17-18].

The Israelites lacked leadership. That is always characteristic of men, or of a generation, that have turned from God. Lack of leadership has definitely characterized our nation for the last twenty-five years. In fact, there has been a lack of leadership in the world for many years.

We need vital leadership, but we cannot seem to find it. This was Israel's experience. Now they are going to turn to a most unusual man for guidance. Under normal circumstances they would not have turned to him at all.

CHAPTER 11

THEME: Jephthah, the ninth judge, and his rash vow

Now Jephthah the Gileadite was a mighty man of valour and he was the son of an harlot: and Gilead begat Jephthah [Jud. 11:1].

The first thing that I would call to your attention is that he is an outstanding leader, but he has this black mark against him: he is illegitimate, the son of a harlot.

And Gilead's wife bare him sons; and his wife's sons grew up, and they thrust out Jephthah, and said unto him, Thou shalt not inherit in our father's house; for thou art the son of a strange woman [Jud. 11:2].

Proverbs 2:16 speaks of "the strange woman" whom the son should beware because harlots were strangers—that is, foreigners. Josephus tells us that Gilead's wife was a Gentile. Jewish writings have called her an Ishmaelite. So Jephthah was the son of a common heathen prostitute. Illegitimacy is a stigma that brands a person from birth, regardless of who he is. This man Jephthah was exiled. He was excommunicated and ostracized. According to Deuteronomy 23:2, the Law of Moses would also bar him from the congregation of the Lord.

Being an illegitimate child is a handicap, to be sure, but many men have overcome it. There are kings, emperors, generals, poets, and popes who have been illegitimate children. William the Conqueror, for example, signed his name "William the Bastard," for that is what he was. That is what Jephthah was also, and he overcame this handicap, as we shall see.

Then Jephthah fled from his brethren, and dwelt in the land of Tob: and there were gathered vain men to Jephthah, and went out with him [Jud. 11:3].

Jephthah had become a leader of a band of desperados. Here is this man with three hurdles to surmount before he can become a leader for his country: he is the son of a harlot; he has been exiled by his brethren; and he is the leader of a despised, rejected group. He is not a very likely man to be used; but, you see, God uses men like this. God moves in mysterious ways, and He chooses men that are despised in this world. God also humbles those whom He intends to use. He humbled Joseph, He humbled Moses, and He humbled David. Our Lord humbled Himself. He is "despised and rejected of men." He is the "Stone which the builders rejected," but which was made the head of the corner. His enemies said, "We will not have this Man reign over us." Yet God has highly exalted Him and given Him a name that is above every name.

There are those today, friend, who claim to be sons of God, but they are not. They are illegitimate in that they have not been born again. You can only become a legitimate son of God by trusting the Lord Jesus Christ.

Jephthah had been an exile, but now he is exalted.

And it came to pass in process of time, that the children of Ammon made war against Israel.

And it was so, that when the children of Ammon made war against Israel, the elders of Gilead went to fetch Jephthah out of the land of Tob:

And they said unto Jephthah, Come, and be our captain, that we may fight with the children of Ammon.

And Jephthah said unto the elders of Gilead, Did not ye hate me, and expel me out of my father's house? and why are ye come unto me now when ye are in distress?

And the elders of Gilead said unto Jephthah, Therefore we turn again to thee now, that thou mayest go with us, and fight against the children of Ammon, and be our head over all the inhabitants of Gilead [Jud. 11:4–8].

The elders of Gilead have made Jephthah a pretty good proposition.

> **And Jephthah said unto the elders of Gilead, If ye bring
> me home again to fight against the children of Ammon,
> and the LORD deliver them before me, shall I be your
> head?**
>
> **And the elders of Gilead said unto Jephthah, The LORD
> be witness between us, if we do not so according to thy
> words [Jud. 11:9–10].**

Jephthah makes things difficult for the elders of Gilead, but they have
to swallow their pride and accept his terms. It was humiliating for the
nation to appeal to this man whom they had exiled. And he makes it
very clear that if he is going to be the judge and deliver them, then he is
going to rule over them. Then he takes charge of things.

> **Then Jephthah went with the elders of Gilead, and the
> people made him head and captain over them: and Jeph-
> thah uttered all his words before the LORD in Mizpeh.**
>
> **And Jephthah sent messengers unto the king of the chil-
> dren of Ammon, saying, What hast thou to do with me,
> that thou art come against me to fight in my land? [Jud.
> 11:11–12].**

If you read the verses that follow this portion of Scripture, you will
find an extended section where Jephthah outlines the way that the Ammonites came into the land. He makes it clear that the land really belonged to the Israelites who gained the land in a legitimate way. The
Ammonites were, of course, attempting not only to drive the Israelites
off the land, but were also trying to exterminate them. The same thing
is happening in the land of Israel today. Especially since 1948 when
Israel once again became a nation, the enemy has been trying to remove them from the land, exterminate them, actually drive them into
the sea. I will not go over this section, but it will pay you to read it for

the simple reason that Jephthah outlines a very sensible basis for Israel's occupation of the land. They had a legitimate claim to it.

> **Howbeit the king of the children of Ammon hearkened not unto the words of Jephthah which he sent him.**
>
> **Then the spirit of the LORD came upon Jephthah, and he passed over Gilead, and Manasseh, and passed over Mizpeh of Gilead, and from Mizpeh of Gilead he passed over unto the children of Ammon [Jud. 11:28–29].**

The king of Ammon totally rejects the paper that Jephthah apparently had sent to him. He said he would not accept what had been said. So Jephthah leads his army against the Ammonites. But when he passes through the land and gets a look at the enemy, he becomes a little fearful. Now he does something that under normal circumstances he probably would not have done. Remember that this man had spent years in exile and then suddenly he is exalted to the highest position in the land. He is made a judge. The natural reaction of a man who is suddenly elevated is excitement. In his excitement he makes a rash promise. Also remember that Jephthah did not have the light that we have today. He was one-half pagan with a heathen background. He did know God but not very well. God did not require him to make a vow.

> **And Jephthah vowed a vow unto the LORD, and said, If thou shalt without fail deliver the children of Ammon into mine hands,**
>
> **Then it shall be, that whatsoever cometh forth of the doors of my house to meet me, when I return in peace from the children of Ammon, shall surely be the LORD's, and I will offer it up for a burnt offering [Jud. 11:30–31].**

His cause was just, and God had given Jephthah every assurance that he would be victorious. This man did not need to make a rash vow like this, because God had not put the victory on that basis. It was the hand of God that had elevated him to this high position. He should have recognized that, since God had brought him that far, He would see him through. In verse 29 of this chapter we were told that the Spirit of the Lord came upon him. He did not need to add anything to that. Can you imagine saying, "Whatever comes out to meet me I will deliver it to the Lord?" After all, suppose it had been a friend or a neighbor. He would have no right to dedicate or offer that individual to the Lord.

> **And Jephthah came to Mizpeh unto his house, and, behold, his daughter came out to meet him with timbrels and with dances: and she was his only child; beside her he had neither son nor daughter.**

> **And it came to pass, when he saw her, that he rent his clothes, and said, Alas, my daughter! thou hast brought me very low, and thou art one of them that trouble me: for I have opened my mouth unto the LORD, and I cannot go back [Jud. 11:34–35].**

Jephthah made a vow to God, and he feels that he cannot retract it.

The question is: did he offer his daughter in sacrifice? Let us look at this situation closely for a moment. The Scripture is silent concerning Jephthah's vow. It does not say whether he was right or wrong. Scripture never finds fault with him. In fact, Hebrews 11:32 says, "And what shall I more say? for the time would fail me to tell of Gedeon, and of Barak, and of Samson, and of Jephthae; of David also, and Samuel, and of the prophets." As you see, Jephthah is mentioned with a very fine group of men.

God's commandment is "Thou shalt not kill" (Exod. 20:13). God also gave rather specific instructions about offering children. We read in Deuteronomy 12:31: "Thou shalt not do so unto the LORD thy God: for every abomination to the LORD, which he hateth, have they done unto their gods; for even their sons and their daughters they have burnt in the fire to their gods." God says, "I won't ask you to do that, and you are *not* to do that, because it is pagan and heathen." God did not permit Abraham to offer Isaac. We need to recognize that fact. The whole point with Abraham and Isaac was how far Abraham was willing to go with God. As it turned out, he was willing to go all the way with God.

Abraham lifted that knife and, as far as he was concerned, Isaac was a
dead boy. But as far as God was concerned, He would not let Abraham
kill his son.

The construction used in the language in verse 31 determines, I
feel, the interpretation. Notice what Jephthah says, ". . . whatsoever
cometh forth of the doors of my house to meet me, when I return in
peace from the children of Ammon, shall surely be the LORD's, and I
will offer it up for a burnt offering." I am going to change the reading of
the last phrase just a little. It can read, "or I will offer up a burnt offering." Now Jephthah said he would do one of two things: he would offer
a burnt offering or he would offer a gift to the Lord.

Did he offer his daughter as a burnt offering? I do not think that he
did. What is meant is that he set her apart to perpetual virginity. So
here is Jephthah—he is illegitimate himself and he has only one
daughter. He wants her to marry so he can have grandchildren. But his
daughter is the one who comes forth through the doors to greet him,
and he offers her up to the Lord. That means that she will never marry.
You say to me, "Can you be sure of that?" Well, listen to what the girl
says.

> And she said unto him, My father, if thou hast opened
> thy mouth unto the LORD, do to me according to that
> which hath proceeded out of thy mouth; forasmuch as
> the LORD hath taken vengeance for thee of thine enemies,
> even of the children of Ammon [Jud. 11:36].

Notice that his daughter was obedient. She said that she would do
whatever he had promised the Lord.

> And she said unto her father, Let this thing be done for
> me: let me alone two months, that I may go up and down
> upon the mountains, and bewail my virginity, I and my
> fellows [Jud. 11:37].

She did not understand his promise to be a burnt offering or sacrifice,
but that she is not going to marry. Those are her intentions, and she is

to bewail the fact of her virginity. She will not be presented as a bride to some man. Her life is to be dedicated to the Lord.

And he said, Go. And he sent her away for two months: and she went with her companions, and bewailed her virginity upon the mountains.

And it came to pass at the end of two months, that she returned unto her father, who did with her according to his vow which he had vowed: and she knew no man. And it was a custom in Israel.

That the daughters of Israel went yearly to lament the daughter of Jephthah the Gileadite four days in a year [Jud. 11:38–40].

This passage tells us that Jephthah's daughter did not get married. Instead she dedicated her life to the Lord. The word *lament* in verse 40 means "to celebrate." Every year for four days Jephthah's daughter was remembered in a special way. She was totally dedicated to the Lord and His service. There is no indication that she was made a human sacrifice. People have argued about this story for years. I am asked that question as much as any other question: "Did Jephthah offer up his daughter in sacrifice?" No, he did not, but that is not the point. God would not have permitted him to offer his daughter in a burnt sacrifice. The significant factor is that Jephthah kept his vow. His vow was something sacred. He did not trifle with it. It was a rash statement, to be sure, but it was not an idle boast. It was not a hollow promise. The Word of God has some severe and sharp things to say relative to making a vow. Notice what the Book of Ecclesiastes has to say about vows. "Be not rash with thy mouth, and let not thine heart be hasty to utter any thing before God: for God is in heaven, and thou upon earth: therefore let thy words be few. When thou vowest a vow unto God, defer not to pay it; for he hath no pleasure in fools: pay that which thou hast vowed. Better is it that thou shouldest not vow, than that thou shouldest vow and not pay" (Eccl. 5:2, 4–5). My friend, you will do well to promise God only what you think you can execute. I am afraid that there are many Christians who go through a little ceremony. Perhaps they go down to an altar after a service, and by lighting a candle they dedicate themselves to God. Some folk dedicate and dedicate themselves until it actually smells to high heaven! God says, "Don't be rash with your mouth." He says that you are a fool if you make a vow to Him carelessly. You might think that over, Christian friend, in the next dedication service you attend. Don't rush down to the altar and offer God everything if you don't mean what you are saying. Jephthah was an illegitimate child. His mother was a harlot. He had a sweet, lovely daughter, and he wanted her to marry and have children. He unwittingly dedicated her to the Lord, but he kept his vow.

Christians today are notorious at making vows and breaking them. I noted this when I first began to move in Christian circles. As a young Christian, I went to a young people's conference and watched eighteen young people go forward and dedicate themselves to the Lord for full-time Christian service. I wouldn't go forward because I did not know whether I could make good my promise. May I say that out of all those who dedicated themselves to the Lord's service that night, not one of them entered full-time service! Have you made a vow to God? If you have, He wants you to keep it. "It is a faithful saying: For if we be dead with him, we shall also live with him: If we suffer, we shall also reign with him: if we deny him, he also will deny us: If we believe not, yet he abideth faithful: he cannot deny himself" (2 Tim 2:11–13). Oh, He keeps His Word. Let us keep our word. "But the Lord is faithful, who shall stablish you, and keep you from evil" (2 Thess. 3:3). My, how wonderful He is, and how foolish we are today! Jephthah should be a lesson to us today.

CHAPTER 12

THEME: Jealousy of Ephraim; Judges Ibzan, Elon, and Abdon

EPHRAIM IS PUNISHED

And the men of Ephraim gathered themselves together, and went northward, and said unto Jephthah, Wherefore passedst thou over to fight against the children of Ammon, and didst not call us to go with thee? we will burn thine house upon thee with fire.

And Jephthah said unto them, I and my people were at great strife with the children of Ammon; and when I called you, ye delivered me not out of their hands.

And when I saw that ye delivered me not, I put my life in my hands, and passed over against the children of Ammon, and the LORD delivered them into my hand: wherefore then are ye come up unto me this day, to fight against me? [Jud. 12:1–3].

We have seen that the men of Ephraim also quarreled with Gideon (8:1) when he didn't summon them to help him rout the Midianites. Now in a hostile way, they demanded that Jephthah give them the reason why he did not ask for their help in the battle. The jealousy of Ephraim was a real infection that led to a defection. Later on, when the kingdom is divided into north and south, you will find out that Ephraim is the center of all of the rebellion. And it goes back to their jealousy.

There is jealousy in the church today. It is one of our greatest problems. Paul said, "Let nothing be done through strife or vainglory; but in lowliness of mind let each esteem other better than themselves" (Phil. 2:3). "Strife and vainglory" can be vanity and envy. These are two things that cause problems in churches today. When I hear some person in a church complain that it is not being run the way he thinks it should be, I wonder if he is jealous. When I find someone who is opposing the preacher all of the time, I suspect there is jealousy behind it.

Jealousy was the problem here. Jephthah had to protect himself. The men of Ephraim were going to burn his house down right over his head!

> Then Jephthah gathered together all the men of Gilead, and fought with Ephraim: and the men of Gilead smote Ephraim, because they said, Ye Gileadites are fugitives of Ephraim among the Ephraimites, and among the Manassites.
>
> And the Gileadites took the passages of Jordan before the Ephraimites: and it was so, that when those Ephraimites which were escaped said, Let me go over; that the men of Gilead said unto him, Art thou an Ephraimite? If he said, Nay;
>
> Then said they unto him, Say now Shibboleth: and he said Sibboleth: for he could not frame to pronounce it right. Then they took him, and slew him at the passages of Jordan: and there fell at that time of the Ephraimites forty and two thousand [Jud. 12:4-6].

The Gileadites were successful in defeating the Ephraimites, and they seized the Jordan fords so that the Ephraimites could not escape. Then they selected a password that would be difficult to pronounce because it contained a consonant which was not in the Ephraimite dialect. The word was *Shibboleth*. If a person's accent was not just right when he pronounced this word, he was in trouble. It is difficult for us to say certain words. *Shibboleth* was a word that was difficult for the Ephraimites to say because they could not put the "h" in it.

> And Jephthah judged Israel six years. Then died Jephthah the Gileadite, and was buried in one of the cities of Gilead [Jud. 12:7].

Jephthah's death ended six eventful years.

IBZAN, THE TENTH JUDGE

The next three judges mentioned were practically zeros. They did nothing. Well, they did something, but they did not judge Israel as they should have done.

And after him Ibzan of Beth-lehem judged Israel.

And he had thirty sons, and thirty daughters, whom he sent abroad, and took in thirty daughters from abroad for his sons. And he judged Israel seven years.

Then died Ibzan, and was buried at Beth-lehem [Jud. 12:8–10].

This judge is from Bethlehem. Bethlehem was one of the cities of Judah in the south. Ibzan had thirty sons and thirty daughters. I would have thought that he would have worked at getting his daughters husbands instead of getting wives for his sons. I suppose that in the seven years that he was judge he did not have time to get his daughters husbands too. He did not have time to judge Israel either. In other words, Ibzan was a man who gave all of his time to his family. There is nothing wrong with that, but it was not what he was called to do.

There is a great deal of nonsense abroad today about the subject of responsibility. I once heard the story of a preacher who was on his way to a speaking engagement and his little son wanted to talk with him. He sat down and talked to his son and missed his speaking engagement. Many people applauded him for that. Well, my friend, that man was breaking an engagement and also he was spoiling a child. You can show love and interest in your children without breaking an engagement. There is a time when certain things have to be put first. I think he would have better served the boy if he had told him, "Your daddy has a speaking engagement and that is important. You would want your daddy to keep that appointment, wouldn't you?" I think the little fellow would have agreed. Then the father could have continued,

"Now when I return, you and I will talk these things over, or tomorrow we can have a chat." That would have done more for the boy than what the father did. All he did was make a spoiled brat out of the youngster, as I see it. I know I sound like a square, but I do not approve of judge Ibzan's actions. He didn't do anything. He is a picture of mediocrity, to be sure.

ELON, THE ELEVENTH JUDGE

And after him Elon, a Zebulonite, judged Israel; and he judged Israel ten years.

And Elon the Zebulonite died, and was buried in Aijalon in the country of Zebulun [Jud. 12:11–12].

These two verses tell us all that we know about Elon. He did nothing—he didn't even have a large family. Apparently all that he did was twiddle his thumbs.

ABDON, THE TWELFTH JUDGE

And after him Abdon the son of Hillel, a Pirathonite, judged Israel.

And he had forty sons and thirty nephews, that rode on threescore and ten ass colts: and he judged Israel eight years.

And Abdon the son of Hillel the Pirathonite died, and was buried in Pirathon in the land of Ephraim, in the mount of the Amalekites [Jud. 12:13–15].

Abdon did nothing except "out-Jair" Jair. Talk about keeping up with the Jones family! As we have seen in chapter 10, Jair had thirty sons—but Abdon had forty sons and thirty nephews besides. It must have been quite a sight to see that man ride out of town with his sons and nephews. You would have seen a parade of Jaguars, Mustangs, Pintos, and Cougars like you had never seen before. They call the little donkey the "mockingbird" or "lark" of the desert because he can really bray. Just think of all of those braying donkeys! That is all Abdon contributed. That isn't much, friend.

We have quickly passed over the last three judges, Ibzan, Elon, and Abdon, because apparently they did nothing constructive as judges.

CHAPTERS 13—16

THEME: *Seventh apostasy; Israel partially delivered through Samson*

FORTY YEARS OF SERVITUDE
UNDER THE PHILISTINES

And the children of Israel did evil again in the sight of the LORD; and the LORD delivered them into the hand of the Philistines forty years [Jud. 13:1].

The repeated apostasy of Israel forms the setting for a time of oppression by the Philistines. The Philistines were probably the worst enemies that Israel had. This time their oppression lasted for forty years.

During this time we come to a judge that we cannot pass over. His name was Samson, and he was one of the most outstanding of the judges. He probably had more glorious opportunity than any man ever had. Everything was propitious for a career and a brilliant future, but he failed. That is the tragedy of this man's life. He came to judge during the seventh apostasy and is, in one sense, the last of the judges. Israel was conquered by the Philistines and was only partially delivered by Samson. The small civil war that began in Jephthah's day got bigger and bigger, and the Book of Judges ends in absolute confusion. During Samson's time of leadership we are given the secret of his success, the secret of his strength, and the secret of his failure. Again, let me repeat, never was a man born with a more glorious opportunity than this man.

BIRTH OF SAMSON, THE THIRTEENTH JUDGE

And there was a certain man of Zorah, of the family of the Danites, whose name was Manoah; and his wife was barren, and bare not [Jud. 13:2].

Zorah was a city between Dan and Judah, several miles west of Jerusalem. Manoah and his wife did not have any children because she was barren. So the birth of Samson was miraculous as was the birth of Isaac, or Joseph, or Benjamin.

> **And the angel of the LORD appeared unto the woman, and said unto her, Behold now, thou art barren, and bearest not: but thou shalt conceive, and bear a son.**
>
> **Now therefore beware, I pray thee, and drink not wine nor strong drink, and eat not any unclean thing:**
>
> **For, lo, thou shalt conceive, and bear a son; and no razor shall come on his head: for the child shall be a Nazarite unto God from the womb: and he shall begin to deliver Israel out of the hand of the Philistines [Jud. 13:3–5].**

Before Samson was born, God marked him out. God raised him up to perform a gigantic task: he was to deliver Israel. The people of Israel were in a bad way because God had delivered them into the hands of the Philistines.

The angel of the Lord that appeared to the mother of Samson told her what her son was to be—a Nazarite. You will recall that back in the Book of Numbers we are told what constituted a Nazarite vow. It was threefold: (1) He was not to touch strong drink or use grapes in any form. Why? Because wine is a symbol in the Scriptures of earthly joy. It is to cheer the heart. The Nazarite was to find his joy in the Lord. Ephesians 5:18 says, "And be not drunk with wine, wherein is excess; but be filled with the Spirit." If we want to please Christ, we, too, are to find our joy in Him. In fact, joy is a fruit of the Holy Spirit—"But the fruit of the Spirit is love, joy, peace, longsuffering, gentleness, goodness, faith, Meekness, temperance: against such there is no law" (Gal. 5:22–23). Joy is one of the fruits the Holy Spirit wants to produce in your life and mine. (2) A Nazarite was not to cut his hair. Now what does that mean? In 1 Corinthians 11:14 Paul says, "Doth not even nature itself teach you, that, if a man have long hair, it is a shame unto him?" The Scripture says that long hair dishonors a man. A Nazarite, however, would be willing to bear the shame of long hair, and that is the reason a razor was not to touch his head. (3) He was not to go near a dead body. There were to be no natural claims upon him. He had to put God first, above his relatives and loved ones. The Lord Jesus said in Luke 14:26–27, "If any man come to me, and hate not his father, and mother, and wife, and children, and brethren, and sisters, yea, and his own life also, he cannot be my disciple. And whosoever doth not bear his cross, and come after me, cannot be my disciple." This simply means that we cannot put *anything* before Christ. This is something that we have lost sight of today.

Samson was a Nazarite. He was God's man, and that was the secret of the success he had. He was raised up for a great purpose, and his success was in God. Unfortunately he never succeeded in performing his God-appointed task. Did you notice what verse 5 said? Samson *began* to deliver Israel out of the hands of the Philistines. Success knocked at his door. He was a beginner, not a finisher. He began to deliver Israel, but he never finished the task.

There are many Christians like that. They make a great beginning, but they do not finish a task. Paul said to the Galatians, "Ye did run well; who did hinder you that ye should not obey the truth?" (Gal. 5:7). They started out with a bang and ended up with a fizzle. Many people begin to read the Bible, but many fall by the wayside. They just begin and don't go on with it. I have been a pastor for forty years, friend, and I have known lots of people who start something and never conclude it. They never finish what they are called to do.

And the woman bare a son, and called his name Samson: and the child grew, and the LORD blessed him.

And the Spirit of the LORD began to move him at times in the camp of Dan between Zorah and Eshtaol [Jud. 13:24–25].

These verses tell us the secret of Samson's strength. Samson's strength was not in his arms, although he killed a thousand Philistines with those arms. His strength was not in his back, although he carried the gates of Gaza on his back, which was a remarkable undertaking. And

Samson's strength was not in his hair, although he was weak when it
was cut. Samson was strong only when the Spirit of God was moving
him. Just cutting his hair off was not actually what weakened him. His
hair was the badge of his Nazarite vow. The Spirit of God was not on
him when his hair was cut. Why? Because he had failed in his vow. He
had not made good.

We see advertisements of body builders which show the man before
and after. The *before* picture always features a little dried up weasel.
After he takes the tonic, we see a great big muscle-bound man. Even
though many people have pictured Samson as a big bruiser, he was
probably one of the worst sissies in or out of the Bible. I think he was a
little, dried-up milquetoast type of man. His name means "little sun."
He had long hair. He was a riddle maker. He played pranks like a
schoolboy. He allowed women to make a fool of him. He was not a he-
man. He was not the strongest man in the Bible. He was the weakest
man. This fellow was tied to his mama's apron strings like a little
sissy, and that is exactly what he was. Then when the Spirit of the Lord
began to move him, he was strong. When the Spirit was not upon him,
he was as weak as water.

The people in Samson's day wanted to know the source of his
strength. They did not realize that God chooses the weak things of this
world to accomplish His purposes. They marveled at Samson, "How
can this little scrawny, milquetoast fellow, perform these feats of tremendous strength?" There was only one explanation—God did it.

SAMSON IS PROMISED A WIFE

It is amazing that the Spirit of God would come upon a man like this.
But it is obvious that God moved through him. I feel that he was a sissy
in every department of his life, and in chapter 14 we begin to see it.

**And Samson went down to Timnath, and saw a woman
in Timnath of the daughters of the Philistines.**

**And he came up, and told his father and his mother, and
said, I have seen a woman in Timnath of the daughters**

of the Philistines: now therefore get her for me to wife
[Jud. 14:1-2].

I submit to you that only a sissy would do a thing like that! Why didn't
he go and talk to the woman and tell her that he loved her and wanted
to marry her? Why didn't he go and talk to her father? In those days
some sort of a business arrangement was always made when it came to
marriage. Why didn't he take care of that himself? Well, he is a sissy,
and mamma and papa had to arrange the marriage for him. This is
Samson.

> Then his father and his mother said unto him, Is there
> never a woman among the daughters of thy brethren, or
> among all my people, that thou goest to take a wife of
> the uncircumcised Philistines? And Samson said unto
> his father, Get her for me; for she pleaseth me well.
>
> But his father and his mother knew not that it was of the
> LORD, that he sought an occasion against the Philistines:
> for at that time the Philistines had dominion over Israel
> [Jud. 14:3-4].

Samson is going to use his marriage as a ruse in order that he might
deliver Israel from the Philistines. He starts off well.

SAMSON SLAYS A LION AND GIVES A RIDDLE

> Then went Samson down, and his father and his mother,
> to Timnath, and came to the vineyards of Timnath: and,
> behold, a young lion roared against him [Jud. 14:5].

We have been told that a Nazarite was to keep away from the grapes,
but not Samson.

> And the spirit of the LORD came mightily upon him, and
> he rent him as he would have rent a kid, and he had

nothing in his hand: but he told not his father or his mother what he had done.

And he went down, and talked with the woman; and she pleased Samson well.

And after a time he returned to take her, and he turned aside to see the carcase of the lion: and, behold, there was a swarm of bees and honey in the carcase of the lion.

And he took thereof in his hands, and went on eating, and came to his father and mother, and he gave them, and they did eat: but he told not them that he had taken the honey out of the carcase of the lion [Jud. 14:6-9].

On his way to Timnath with his parents, Samson was attacked by a lion. The Spirit of the Lord came upon him during this time of emergency, and he killed the lion with his bare hands. During another trip Samson went to look at the carcass of the lion and discovered a swarm of bees and honey in it. He scooped the honey out with his hands and ate it. He also gave some to his parents, but he did not tell them where he got it. Remember that having contact with a carcass was a violation of the Nazarite law.

So his father went down unto the woman: and Samson made there a feast; for so used the young men to do.

And it came to pass, when they saw him, that they brought thirty companions to be with him.

And Samson said unto them, I will now put forth a riddle unto you: if ye can certainly declare it me within the seven days of the feast, and find it out, then I will give you thirty sheets and thirty change of garments:

But if ye cannot declare it me, then shall ye give me thirty sheets and thirty change of garments. And they said unto him, Put forth thy riddle, that we may hear it.

And he said unto them, Out of the eater came forth meat, and out of the strong came forth sweetness. And they could not in three days expound the riddle [Jud. 14:10–14].

As was the custom, Samson put on a marriage feast. The feast was held at the bride's home. And all of the guests were Philistines. Riddles were a form of entertainment in those days, and Samson gave the guests a riddle. He gave them seven days in which to find the answer. If they guessed the riddle, then Samson would give them thirty linen garments and thirty cloaks. If they failed to guess the answer to his riddle, then they would have to give him thirty linen garments and thirty cloaks. Without knowing about the slain lion and the hive of bees in the carcass, there was no way the thirty guests could solve Samson's riddle.

SAMSON IS DECEIVED AND SLAYS
THIRTY PHILISTINES

And it came to pass on the seventh day, that they said unto Samson's wife, Entice thy husband, that he may declare unto us the riddle, lest we burn thee and thy father's house with fire: have ye called us to take that we have? is it not so?

And Samson's wife wept before him, and said, Thou dost but hate me, and lovest me not: thou hast put forth a riddle unto the children of my people, and hast not told it me. And he said unto her, Behold, I have not told it my father nor my mother, and shall I tell it thee?

And she wept before him the seven days, while their feast lasted: and it came to pass on the seventh day, that

> he told her, because she lay sore upon him: and she told
> the riddle to the children of her people.
>
> And the men of the city said unto him on the seventh day
> before the sun went down. What is sweeter than honey?
> and what is stronger than a lion? And he said unto
> them, If ye had not plowed with my heifer, ye had not
> found out my riddle [Jud. 14:15–18].

The Philistines appealed to Samson's wife to help them find out the answer to the riddle. If she did not find out what his secret was, they threatened to burn down her father's house with her in it. Now the strongest weapon that a woman has is her tears, and Samson's wife turned hers on for seven days. I want to tell you that a woman who weeps for seven straight days, and at every meal, gets a little tiresome. Finally he had to give in and tell her the answer to the riddle. He was good at making wisecracks, too. He knew where these men got the answer to the riddle. Samson said, "If ye had not plowed with my heifer, ye had not found out my riddle." In other words, "You got the answer from my wife."

> And the spirit of the LORD came upon him, and he went
> down to Ashkelon, and slew thirty men of them, and
> took their spoil, and gave change of garments unto them
> which expounded the riddle. And his anger was kin-
> dled, and he went up to his father's house [Jud. 14:19].

The Spirit of the Lord came upon Samson and he went down south to Ashkelon—Ashkelon is way down in the south. There he killed thirty men in order to get thirty changes of raiment that he needed to pay off his wager. Samson left in a pout. Notice that he doesn't take his wife with him. He is angry with her for giving away his riddle.

> But Samson's wife was given to his companion, whom
> he had used as his friend [Jud. 14:20].

So the father of the girl gives her to the best man at the wedding!

SAMSON BURNS THE PHILISTINE CROPS

But it came to pass within a while after, in the time of wheat harvest, that Samson visited his wife with a kid; and he said, I will go in to my wife into the chamber. But her father would not suffer him to go in.

And her father said, I verily thought that thou hadst utterly hated her; therefore I gave her to thy companion: is not her younger sister fairer than she? take her, I pray thee, instead of her [Jud. 15:1–2].

After Samson's anger subsided, he went to visit his wife and brought a kid as a present. Her father informed Samson that he thought Samson no longer wanted her and so he had given her to his friend. Samson did not like this, of course.

And Samson said concerning them, Now shall I be more blameless than the Philistines, though I do them a displeasure.

And Samson went and caught three hundred foxes, and took firebrands, and turned tail to tail, and put a firebrand in the midst between two tails.

And when he had set the brands on fire, he let them go into the standing corn of the Philistines, and burnt up both the shocks, and also the standing corn, with the vineyards and olives [Jud. 15:3–5].

Samson apparently felt justified in vengeance on the Philistines. He caught three hundred foxes, tied their tails together and then tied a torch on the tails, set them on fire, and let the animals loose in the fields. Of course these foxes would really take out on a run, and they would scatter the firebrands everywhere. Actually, friend, this entire episode is like a prank a juvenile would play! Samson certainly doesn't look like God's man here!

> Then the Philistines said, Who hath done this? And they answered, Samson, the son-in-law of the Timnite, because he had taken his wife, and given her to his companion. And the Philistines came up, and burnt her and her father with fire.
>
> And Samson said unto them, Though ye have done this, yet will I be avenged of you, and after that I will cease.
>
> And he smote them hip and thigh with a great slaughter: and he went down and dwelt in the top of the rock Etam [Jud. 15:6–8].

Notice that this is personal. This has nothing to do with his commission from God to deliver Israel from the Philistines. He is just avenging himself. His actions had nothing to do with delivering Israel. His revenge was personal.

SAMSON SLAYS ONE THOUSAND PHILISTINES

After smiting the Philistines with a great slaughter, Samson really had the enemy stirred up. They began looking for him, so he let his own people bind him with ropes in order to protect them from the Philistines.

> And when he came unto Lehi, the Philistines shouted against him: and the spirit of the LORD came mightily upon him, and the cords that were upon his arms became as flax that was burnt with fire, and his bands loosed from off his hands [Jud. 15:14].

The men of Judah took Samson, their prisoner, to Lehi which was occupied by the Philistines. The enemy was overjoyed to see Samson being brought to them bound. Then he broke the bands as if they were nothing. Again we see the strength of this man—but not his own strength.

And he found a new jawbone of an ass, and put forth his
hand, and took it, and slew a thousand men therewith
[Jud. 15:15].

Samson grabbed the closest weapon, which was the jawbone of a donkey, and attacked the enemy. He killed one thousand of them. Notice
the strength of this man. He could never have done such a thing in his
own power of course; it was the Spirit of the Lord upon him that
enabled him to do it. He is beginning to deliver Israel. If only he had
kept that goal before him! But he did not, as we shall see in the next
chapter.

SAMSON'S MORAL FRAILTY

Then went Samson to Gaza, and saw there an harlot,
and went in unto her.

And it was told the Gazites, saying, Samson is come
hither. And they compassed him in, and laid wait for
him all night in the gate of the city, and were quiet all
the night, saying, In the morning, when it is day, we
shall kill him [Jud. 16:1–2].

What a playboy Samson was! The men of the city locked up the city
and they said, "We'll get him in the morning."

And Samson lay till midnight, and arose at midnight,
and took the doors of the gate of the city, and the two
posts, and went away with them, bar and all, and put
them upon his shoulders, and carried them up to the top
of an hill that is before Hebron [Jud. 16:3].

Samson got up at midnight and found the gates of the city locked. So
what did he do? He took the gate, posts, bar and all, put them on his
shoulders, and carried them away to the top of a hill that is before
Hebron. That would have been about forty miles away. What he did

sounds like a prank of a teenager or the trick of a college student. This boy Samson never did grow up. He has been called to deliver Israel with his mighty power, but all he does is use it for his personal advantage.

SAMSON AND DELILAH

And it came to pass afterward, that he loved a woman in the valley of Sorek, whose name was Delilah [Jud. 16:4].

That is the story of Samson. That is the downfall of Samson. That is the big failure in his life. That is the weak point in his life—"he loved a woman." No man falls suddenly into sin—he does it gradually.

There was a bank president in my congregation when I pastored a church in Texas. This man went with me to the local jail to hand out tracts and talk to prisoners. Outwardly he was an outstanding man. One day he disappeared. He had gone on vacation. Suddenly the bank began to miss money. They could not believe that he had taken it. They tried to account for the loss in every other way, but they could not. They finally decided that he must be the one who took the money, and when he did not return from vacation, they began to search for him. After a complete investigation, they discovered that he had been taking money for years. No man falls suddenly into sin.

One of the greatest sins that destroys many a man today is this matter of illicit sex. That was Samson's sin—"he loved a woman whose name was Delilah." As far as we know, he made no attempt to marry her.

And the lords of the Philistines came up unto her, and said unto her, Entice him, and see wherein his great strength lieth, and by what means we may prevail against him, that we may bind him to afflict him: and we will give thee every one of us eleven hundred pieces of silver.

And Delilah said to Samson, Tell me, I pray thee, wherein thy great strength lieth, and wherewith thou mightest be bound to afflict thee.

And Samson said unto her, If they bind me with seven green withs that were never dried, then shall I be weak, and be as another man [Jud. 16:5-7].

You may be sure that Delilah was more interested in the silver than she was in Samson. Once again the Philistine leaders had found a way to get to Samson.

Notice that he teases her at first. He begins to give her answers, but they are wrong answers. He broke the cords with no effort at all. Still his strength was not known.

And Delilah said unto Samson, Behold, thou hast mocked me, and told me lies: now tell me, I pray thee, wherewith thou mightest be bound.

And he said unto her, If they bind me fast with new ropes that never were occupied, then shall I be weak, and be as another man [Jud. 16:10-11].

Again he is playing with her; he is kidding her along. He allowed her to tie him up with ropes. Then when she cried, "The Philistines are upon thee, Samson," he broke the ropes like they were a thread. Now Delilah is really exasperated. She is frustrated with her boy friend.

And Delilah said unto Samson, Hitherto thou hast mocked me, and told me lies: tell me wherewith thou mightest be bound. And he said unto her, If thou weavest the seven locks of my head with the web.

And she fastened it with the pin, and said unto him, The Philistines be upon thee, Samson. And he awaked out of his sleep, and went away with the pin of the beam, and with the web [Jud. 16:13-14].

Now Samson is beginning to weaken. May I say to you, friend, this is the beginning of the end of this man. He is getting close to the truth now as he mentions his hair. But he is still teasing with her, and when she says "The Philistines are upon thee, Samson," he picks the whole thing up and walks away with it.

> And she said unto him, How canst thou say, I love thee, when thine heart is not with me? thou hast mocked me these three times, and hast not told me wherein thy great strength lieth.
>
> And it came to pass, when she pressed him daily with her words, and urged him, so that his soul was vexed unto death;
>
> That he told her all his heart, and said unto her, There hath not come a razor upon mine head; for I have been a Nazarite unto God from my mother's womb: if I be shaven, then my strength will go from me, and I shall become weak, and be like any other man [Jud. 16:15–17].

This time Delilah tells Samson that if he *really* loved her he would tell her the secret of his strength. So Samson told her that he was a Nazarite. Long hair, as you remember, was a badge of this vow. His strength was not in his hair but in the Spirit of God who came upon him. Delilah sees what a fool he really is—and he is a fool.

> And when Delilah saw that he had told her all his heart, she sent and called for the lords of the Philistines, saying, Come up this once, for he hath shewed me all his heart. Then the lords of the Philistines came up unto her, and brought money in their hand.
>
> And she made him sleep upon her knees; and she called for a man, and she caused him to shave off the seven locks of his head; and she began to afflict him, and his strength went from him.

> And she said, The Philistines be upon thee, Samson.
> And he awoke out of his sleep, and said, I will go out as
> at other times before, and shake myself. And he wist not
> that the LORD was departed from him [Jud. 16:18-20].

When Samson went to sleep, Delilah had one of the Philistines come
in and shave off his hair. Then for the fourth time Delilah cried out,
"The Philistines be upon thee, Samson!" This is the tragic time in the
life of Samson. He awoke out of his sleep, thinking he would do as he
had done before, but "he knew not that the Lord was departed from
him." Friend, the strength was not in his hair; the strength was in the
Spirit of the Lord who was upon him.

Friend, our spiritual strength today is not in ceremonies or in rit-
uals. The strength of the believer is always in the Spirit of God—
always.

Samson, called to be a judge for his people, called to deliver his
people from the oppression of the Philistines, is a carnal man. Now
Ichabod (meaning "the glory is departed") is written over his life. He
never raised an army. He never won a battle. He never rallied the men of
Israel to him. Sex was the ruin of this man—this man who was chosen
by God!

> But the Philistines took him, and put out his eyes, and
> brought him down to Gaza, and bound him with fetters
> of brass; and he did grind in the prison house.
>
> Howbeit the hair of his head began to grow again after
> he was shaven.
>
> Then the lords of the Philistines gathered them together
> for to offer a great sacrifice unto Dagon their god, and to
> rejoice: for they said, Our god hath delivered Samson
> our enemy into our hand [Jud. 16:21-23].

Now we are coming to the tragic end of this man. After the Philistines
captured Samson, they put out his eyes—blinded him—then forced
him to do the work of a beast of burden in the prison. While he was in

prison, his hair began to grow. He now has become a very repentant man.

The Philistines, of course, ascribe their victory over Samson to their god Dagon and hold a feast to celebrate.

SAMSON IS AVENGED IN HIS DEATH

And it came to pass, when their hearts were merry, that they said, Call for Samson, that he may make us sport. And they called for Samson out of the prison house; and he made them sport: and they set him between the pillars.

And Samson said unto the lad that held him by the hand, Suffer me that I may feel the pillars whereupon the house standeth, that I may lean upon them.

Now the house was full of men and women; and all the lords of the Philistines were there; and there were upon the roof about three thousand men and women, that beheld while Samson made sport [Jud. 16:25–27].

To make their victory celebration complete, the Philistines have Samson brought from the prison. Then they make a fool of him. About three thousand men and women watch Samson being tormented.

And Samson called unto the Lord, and said, O Lord God, remember me, I pray thee, and strengthen me, I pray thee, only this once, O God, that I may be at once avenged of the Philistines for my two eyes.

And Samson took hold of the two middle pillars upon which the house stood, and on which it was borne up, of the one with his right hand, and of the other with his left.

And Samson said, Let me die with the Philistines. And he bowed himself with all his might; and the house fell

upon the lords, and upon all the people that were therein. So the dead which he slew at his death were more than they which he slew in his life.

Then his brethren and all the house of his father came down, and took him, and brought him up, and buried him between Zorah and Eshtaol in the buryingplace of Manoah his father. And he judged Israel twenty years [Jud. 16:28–31].

Samson was a failure. He *began* to deliver Israel—but he failed. He preferred to play with sin until the Spirit of God departed from him. Three significant verses tell his story:

1. Secret of Samson's *success*—
   For, lo, thou shalt conceive, and bear a son; and no razor shall come on his head; for the child shall be a Nazarite unto God from the womb: and he shall begin to deliver Israel out of the hand of the Philistines (Jud. 13:5).
2. Secret of Samson's *strength*—
   And the Spirit of the Lord began to move him at times in the camp of Dan between Zorah and Eshtaol (Jud. 13:25).
3. Secret of Samson's *failure*—
   And she said, The Philistines be upon thee, Samson. And he awoke out of his sleep, and said, I will go out as at other times before, and shake myself. And he wist not that the Lord was departed from him (Jud. 16:20).

Note the parallel between the life of Samson and that of Jesus Christ:

Comparison: 1. Both births were foretold by an angel.
2. Both were separated to God from the womb.
3. Both were Nazarites.
4. Both moved in the power of the Holy Spirit.

5. Both were rejected by their people.
6. Both destroyed (or will destroy) their enemies.

Contrast:
1. Samson lived a life of sin; Jesus' life was sinless.
2. Samson at the time of death prayed, "O God, that I may be at once avenged of the Philistines for my two eyes." Jesus prayed, "Father, forgive them; for they know not what they do."
3. In death, Samson's arms were outstretched in wrath; In death, Jesus' arms were outstretched in love.
4. Samson died. Jesus Christ lives!

CHAPTERS 17 AND 18

THEME: Religious apostasy—the temple

RELIGIOUS CONFUSION IN ISRAEL

In chapters 17—21 we have presented the philosophy of history that was mentioned at the beginning of this book. We have seen it illustrated in Judges as the hoop of history rolls over and over. It starts with Israel in the place of blessing. They are serving God. Then there is a departure from God and they do evil. They follow their own way. Then they are sold into slavery. In their slavery and servitude they cry out to God for deliverance. Then they turn to God and repent. Then God raises up judges to deliver them. Then Israel comes back to the place of blessing and becomes a nation that serves God. Just when everything is back in order, they lapse into sin and turn from God again. Altogether Israel went through seven apostasies. This gives us the philosophy of history. Every nation goes down in this order: (1) religious apostasy; (2) moral awfulness; (3) political anarchy. Deterioration begins in the temple, then to the home, and finally to the state. That is the way a nation falls.

This period of apostasy began in the tribe of Dan in their desire to enlarge their borders. It was another lapse into idolatry. It all can be traced to the home of Micah and his mother who spoiled him. The priest, hired by Micah to tend his idols, advised Dan to proceed with a selfish plan. This was the sweet talk of a hired preacher.

IDOLATRY IN EPHRAIM

And there was a man of mount Ephraim, whose name was Micah.

And he said unto his mother, The eleven hundred shekels of silver that were taken from thee, about which thou cursedst, and spakest of also in mine ears, behold,

**the silver is with me; I took it. And his mother said,
Blessed be thou of the Lord, my son [Jud. 17:1-2].**

Micah is an example of a spoiled brat. He is a mama's boy. He knew
that his mother had been saving some money, and he decided to steal
it. His mother, not knowing who stole the money, pronounced a curse
on the thief. So he confessed to being the thief, and instead of his
mama turning him across her knee and applying the board of education to the seat of knowledge, she congratulated him. She said,
"Blessed be thou of the Lord, my son."

> **And when he had restored the eleven hundred shekels of
> silver to his mother, his mother said, I had wholly dedi-
> cated the silver unto the Lord from my hand for my son,
> to make a graven image and a molten image: now there-
> fore I will restore it unto thee [Jud. 17:3].**

When Micah returned the money to his mother, she told him that she
had dedicated that money to the Lord to make a graven image and a
molten image. You see, they have gone off into idolatry! So she turns
around and gives it back to him. You know, there are a lot of Christians
today that are just that inconsistent. She was dedicating the money to
the Lord but using it to make an idol! Many groups take up an offering
and say it is for the Lord, then use most of it for the church social on
Friday night. They say the money is dedicated to the Lord, but actually
it is honoring the god of pleasure.

> **And the man Micah had an house of gods, and made an
> ephod, and teraphim, and consecrated one of his sons,
> who became his priest.**

> **In those days there was no king in Israel, but every man
> did that which was right in his own eyes [Jud. 17:5-6].**

Micah had a house of gods. His mother provided the silver for the
idols, and Micah provided a shrine for them. He also made an ephod

and teraphim to complete the furnishings of the shrine. Then, to top it all off, he consecrated one of his sons to be his priest. They had come to the place where "every man did that which was right in his own eyes."

> **And there was a young man out of Beth-lehem-judah of the family of Judah, who was a Levite, and he sojourned there.**
>
> **And the man departed out of the city from Beth-lehem-judah to sojourn where he could find a place: and he came to mount Ephraim to the house of Micah, as he journeyed.**
>
> **And Micah said unto him, Whence comest thou? And he said unto him, I am a Levite of Beth-lehem-judah, and I go to sojourn where I may find a place.**
>
> **And Micah said unto him, Dwell with me, and be unto me a father and a priest, and I will give thee ten shekels of silver by the year, and a suit of apparel, and thy victuals. So the Levite went in [Jud. 17:7–10].**

It must have bothered Micah a little that he had made his son a priest. So, when this unemployed itinerant preacher came by, Micah hired him. This Levite from Beth-lehem-judah became his private family priest. Here is a priest who is like a hired preacher who becomes a messenger boy of a church board or of a little group. God have mercy on the church that has this kind of a preacher. This Levite has now become a priest and has a house full of idols.

> **And the Levite was content to dwell with the man; and the young man was unto him as one of his sons.**
>
> **And Micah consecrated the Levite; and the young man became his priest, and was in the house of Micah.**

Then said Micah, Now know I that the Lord will do me good, seeing I have a Levite to my priest [Jud. 17:11–13].

This chapter is certainly a revelation of the low spiritual ebb to which the nation Israel had come. Here is a man who thinks just because he has a Levite for his preacher that that is all he needs. How tragic is that kind of thinking. Yet Micah expected the blessing of God upon him. And how many people are like that today?

IDOLATRY IN DAN

The Danites had been assigned territory that was occupied by the mighty Philistines. They felt that they needed more room in which to live. There was no king in Israel. It was a time of utter confusion. There was no leadership.

In those days there was no king in Israel: and in those days the tribe of the Danites sought them an inheritance to dwell in; for unto that day all their inheritance had not fallen unto them among the tribes of Israel [Jud. 18:1].

You will recall in the Book of Joshua that none of the tribes took possession of all the land that was coming to them. That certainly was true of the tribe of Dan way in the north. The Danites had a real problem. In fact, it was so bad they took to the hills.

And the children of Dan sent of their family five men from their coasts, men of valour, from Zorah, and from Eshtaol, to spy out the land, and to search it; and they said unto them, Go, search the land: who when they came to mount Ephraim, to the house of Micah, they lodged there [Jud. 18:2].

These men went out to see what territory the tribe of Dan could take in order to extend and expand the borders of their tribe. During their travels they came to the house of Micah.

> **When they were by the house of Micah, they knew the voice of the young man the Levite: and they turned in thither, and said unto him, Who brought thee hither? and what makest thou in this place? and what hast thou here?**

> **And he said unto them, Thus and thus dealeth Micah with me, and hath hired me, and I am his priest [Jud. 18:3–4].**

This man is nothing but a hired preacher. (God have mercy on the church that has a hired preacher who chooses to be a messenger boy for a little group rather than to preach and teach the Word of God, without fear, without favoritism, and without compromise.) This Levite has compromised. This is a period of compromise, corruption, and confusion, which are the marks of apostasy at any time. We are in a state of apostasy today. The church has compromised. It is in a state of corruption and confusion. Our problem is that it is not returning to its authority, which is the Word of God, and the Lord Jesus Christ who is revealed in the Word of God.

> **And they said unto him, Ask counsel, we pray thee, of God, that we may know whether our way which we go shall be prosperous.**

> **And the priest said unto them, Go in peace: before the LORD is your way wherein ye go [Jud. 18:5–6].**

This is the sweet talk of a hired preacher who says what people want to hear. The five men left and thought what the Levite told them was great.

> And they said, Arise, that we may go up against them:
> for we have seen the land, and, behold, it is very good:
> and are ye still? be not slothful to go, and to enter to
> possess the land.
>
> When ye go, ye shall come unto a people secure, and to
> a large land: for God hath given it into your hands; a
> place where there is no want of any thing that is in the
> earth.
>
> And there went from thence of the family of the Danites,
> out of Zorah and out of Eshtaol, six hundred men ap-
> pointed with weapons of war [Jud. 18:9–11].

A good report is brought back by the spies who suggest that the Danites should possess Laish. So a party of six hundred warriors is
formed, and they take with them their families, and possessions. On
the way back to Laish, they stop by Micah's house and rob him of his
idols and his priest. Then the Danites capture Laish, burn it, rebuild it,
and live in it. They rename the city Dan.

> And the children of Dan set up the graven image: and
> Jonathan, the son of Gershom, the son of Manasseh, he
> and his sons were priests to the tribe of Dan until the
> day of the captivity of the land.
>
> And they set them up Micah's graven image, which he
> made, all the time that the house of God was in Shiloh
> [Jud. 18:30–31].

Here is a picture of real apostasy, friend. Who is Jonathan? He happens to be the grandson of Moses! These people had gone a long way from
God. Remember that Moses had said, speaking for the Lord, "Thou
shalt have no other gods before me. Thou shalt not make unto thee any
graven image, or any likeness of any thing that is in heaven above, or
that is in the earth beneath, or that is in the water under the earth"
(Exod. 20:3–4). And here is Moses' grandson, a priest with an idol!
This is tragic.

When I was a young man studying for the ministry, I was shocked to learn some of the things that were going on within the organized church. Because I had not been brought up in the church, it was a new world and a new life for me. I was deeply impressed with the life and ministry of Dwight L. Moody and considered him a real saint of God—which he *was*, by the way. Then a man who knew him and knew his family told me, "One of his sons holds an office in the most liberal organization in this country." During those early days nothing hurt me as that did. I just couldn't understand how a son of a man like Moody could depart from the Gospel of Jesus Christ and from the integrity and inerrancy of the Word of God!

My friend, apostasy is an *awful* thing. And a nation's problems begin with religious apostasy. This is what happened to the nation of Israel. Here we see Moses' grandson serving as priest with Micah's graven image!

CHAPTER 19

THEME: Moral awfulness—the home

As we have seen in the preceding section, the downfall of a people begins with religious apostasy. From there it moves on to the second stage, which is moral awfulness. This is graphically illustrated in the frightful episode which concludes the Book of Judges. It centers about the tribe of Benjamin. This tribe engaged in gross immorality which led to civil war. It began with the men of Benjamin abusing and finally murdering a Levite's concubine. The other tribes try to exterminate the tribe of Benjamin. This period ends in total national corruption and confusion and with this the Book of Judges concludes: "In those days there was no king in Israel: every man did that which was right in his own eyes" (Jud. 21:25).

> **And it came to pass in those days, when there was no king in Israel, that there was a certain Levite sojourning on the side of mount Ephraim, who took to him a concubine out of Beth-lehem-judah.**
>
> **And his concubine played the whore against him, and went away from him unto her father's house to Bethlehem-judah, and was there four whole months [Jud. 19:1–2].**

These two verses give us another insight into the life of the children of Israel of that day, and it is a good illustration of Romans chapters 1—3. Can you imagine a Levite marrying a woman like that? Well, he did, and she played the harlot, left him, and went back to her father's house. This Levite followed her, was warmly received by her father, and stayed several days. Then the Levite and his concubine left and headed northward. They stayed one night in Gibeah, a city of the Benjamites. An old man who was also from mount Ephraim and was sojourning in Gibeah offered them hospitality. That night, while they were being entertained by their host, some men of the city demanded (as was done in Sodom before its destruction) the Levite for their homosexual gratification. Believing it would mean final death for him, he gave them instead his concubine. They abused her all night and absolutely caused her death by raping her. This horrible act sounds like something that could have happened in our country—does it not? In fact, the parallel to our contemporary society is quite striking as you read through this section.

The Levite was really wrought up by this crime, and what he did reveals how low they were in that day. He took her and cut her up in pieces, then sent a piece to each tribe with a message of what had taken place!

The reaction of the rest of the nation to this outrage is recorded in the next two chapters.

CHAPTERS 20 AND 21

THEME: Political anarchy—the state

Following religious apostasy, then moral awfulness, the next step downward in the life of Israel (and of every nation) is political anarchy. We see this in the last two chapters of the Book of Judges.

When the tribes of Israel received a part of this dismembered woman with the message of what had taken place in Gibeah, they were incensed against the tribe of Benjamin. They believed the law should be enforced. In that respect they had not sunk as low as we have today in our philosophy that lawlessness should be permitted and we should have as little law as possible. They gave Benjamin an opportunity to deliver up the offenders, but instead Benjamin declared war against the other eleven tribes! So the tribes assembled together and came against Benjamin.

> Then all the children of Israel went out, and the congregation was gathered together as one man, from Dan even to Beer-sheba, with the land of Gilead, unto the LORD in Mizpeh.
>
> And the chief of all the people, even of all the tribes of Israel, presented themselves in the assembly of the people of God, four hundred thousand footmen that drew sword [Jud. 20:1–2].

Apparently the tribe of Benjamin had a tremendous army. We are given an interesting sidelight here:

> Among all this people there were seven hundred chosen men lefthanded; every one could sling stones at an hair breadth, and not miss [Jud. 20:16].

I heard a liberal speak for fifteen minutes one time on the fact that David could not have been accurate enough to hit Goliath on the forehead. Consider this verse. These men were as accurate in that day with their slings as we are today with our missiles. If they could get in the range of a slingshot, it would be fatal for anyone. These left-handed men could split a hair!

This same liberal said that the reason David picked up five stones was so that he would have a reserve supply in case he missed with the first stone. Well, that liberal was wrong. Goliath had four sons in the army of the Philistines, and David had a stone for each one of them. David knew how accurate he was.

Now the men of Benjamin were overcome by sheer numbers. In fact, the tribe of Benjamin was almost destroyed.

> **And there fell of Benjamin eighteen thousand men; all these were men of valour.**
>
> **And they turned and fled toward the wilderness unto the rock of Rimmon: and they gleaned of them in the highways five thousand men; and pursued hard after them unto Gidom, and slew two thousand men of them.**
>
> **So that all which fell that day of Benjamin were twenty and five thousand men that drew the sword; all these were men of valour [Jud. 20:44–46].**

The people in the tribe of Benjamin were judged because of their gross immorality. What a tragic thing it was for so many to die. This was the favorite tribe. Benjamin, you will recall, was the youngest son of old Jacob, and a favorite son. Benjamin was the one for whom Judah was willing to lay down his life. He occupied a place next to Judah.

Unfortunately gross immorality had taken place and had set tribe against tribe and class against class. Then what happened? It led to political anarchy. First there was religious apostasy in the temple, then moral awfulness in the home, and finally political anarchy in the state. These are the steps that any nation takes that goes down.

The final chapter in the Book of Judges deals with the mourning for Israel's lost tribe and the provision the people made for its future.

The slaughter of the Benjamites caused Israel to be faced with a new problem. Almost the entire tribe of Benjamin had been destroyed, and the other tribes vowed not to let their daughters marry any of the few remaining Benjamites. Exactly *how* was the tribe of Benjamin going to be preserved? Before the war, the Israelites had made another vow. They said that any who refused to come to Mizpeh and fight would be put to death. They found out that the men of Jabesh-gilead had not responded to the appeal, and so the command went out for twelve thousand men of Israel to kill the males of Jabesh-gilead, marry the women, and bring the virgins back to the camp at Shiloh. These virgins then became wives to four hundred Benjamites. A means was also found to get wives for the remaining Benjamites and to rebuild the cities that had been destroyed in the fighting.

This period ends in total national corruption and confusion. The final verse concludes the sordid story of the Book of Judges:

In those days there was no king in Israel: every man did that which was right in his own eyes [Jud. 21:25].

Here in this twentieth century the heads of state would do well to study the Book of Judges. Back in 1928, when the depression first began, a brief editorial appeared in the staid *Wall Street Journal,* which went something like this:

What America needs today is not Government controls, industrial expansion, or a bumper corn crop; America needs to return to the day when grandpa took the team out of the field in the early afternoon on Wednesday in order to hitch them to the old spring wagon into which grandma put all of the children after she washed their faces shining clean; and they drove off to prayer meeting in the little white church at the crossroads underneath the oak trees, where everyone believed the Bible, trusted Christ, and loved one another.

Where did our trouble begin? Because our trouble is primarily spiritual, it actually goes back to the church. The church went into apostasy. Then our problems centered in the home with the drug problem and the generation gap. Trouble has now moved into political circles, and we have anarchy. People say, "If we could just change this or that and put in this party or that party, everything would be fine." All of this is perfect nonsense. What we need today is to get back to a spiritual foundation. That is where we went off the track, and that is where our troubles began. We have seen in the Book of Judges the philosophy of history, and the hoop of history is still rolling. Frankly, I am disturbed because it has never changed. We today are in the midst of political anarchy. God have mercy on America!

BIBLIOGRAPHY
(Recommended for Further Study)

Davis, John J. *Conquest and Crisis—Studies in Joshua, Judges, and Ruth.* Grand Rapids, Michigan: Baker Book House, 1969.

Enns, Paul P. *Joshua.* Grand Rapids, Michigan: Zondervan Publishing House, 1981.

Enns, Paul P. *Judges.* Grand Rapids, Michigan: Zondervan Publishing House, 1982.

Epp, Theodore H. *Joshua—Victorious by Faith.* Lincoln, Nebraska: Back to the Bible Broadcast, 1968. (Devotional)

Gaebelein, Arno C. *The Annotated Bible,* Vol. 2. Neptune, New Jersey: Loizeaux Brothers, 1917.

Grant, F. W. *Numerical Bible,* Vol. 2. Neptune, New Jersey: Loizeaux Brothers, 1891.

Gray, James M. *Synthetic Bible Studies.* Westwood, New Jersey: Fleming H. Revell Co., 1906.

Ironside, H. A. *Addresses on the Book of Joshua.* Neptune, New Jersey: Loizeaux Brothers, 1950.

Jamieson, Robert; Fausset, A. R.; and Brown, D. *Commentary on the Bible.* 3 Vols. Grand Rapids, Michigan: Wm. B. Eerdmans Publishing Co., 1945.

Jensen, Irving L. *Joshua, Rest—Land Won.* Chicago, Illinois: Moody Press, 1966.

Jensen, Irving L. *Joshua, A Self-Study Guide.* Chicago, Illinois: Moody Press, 1968.

Jensen, Irving L. *Judges & Ruth, A Self-Study Guide.* Chicago, Illinois: Moody Press, 1968.

Lewis, Arthur. *Judges and Ruth*. Chicago, Illinois: Moody Press, 1979.

McGee, J. Vernon. *Ruth, The Romance of Redemption*. Pasadena, California: Thru the Bible Books, 1943.

Mackintosh, C. H. *The Mackintosh Treasury: Miscellaneous Writings*. Neptune, New Jersey: Loizeaux, n.d.

Meyer, F. B. *Joshua, and the Land of Promise*. Fort Washington, Pennsylvania: Christian Literature Crusade, n.d. (A rich devotional study)

Pink, Arthur W. *Gleanings in Joshua*. Chicago, Illinois: Moody Press, 1964.

Redpath, Alan. *Victorious Christian Living*. Westwood, New Jersey: Fleming H. Revell Co., 1955. (Devotional studies in Joshua)

Ridout, Samuel. *Lectures on the Book of Judges & Ruth*. Neptune, New Jersey: Loizeaux Brothers, n.d. (Excellent)